DESIGN TO SURVIVE

DESIGN TO SURVIVE

9 WAYS AN IKEA APPROACH CAN FIX HEALTH CARE & SAVE LIVES

"It was a stroke of genius to apply the IKEA model to health care, since this forward-looking company revolutionized home furnishings by creating an efficient partnership between retailer and customer in a smart, cost-effective manner, by design…[Mastors'] passionate plea for simplicity and common sense deserves notice. There's so much good advice here that I have made this book mandatory reading for our design staff. And for a patient, the book's advice might just save your life."

—From the Foreword, by Award-Winning
Architect and Designer **Michael Graves**

"A tremendous toolkit for getting safe care…we are all patients at some point. Mastors' is a wonderfully pragmatic mind, applying common sense solutions to a mammoth problem…there is a lot we as physicians can learn from her. I highly recommend this well-written book"

—Marty Makary *MD, Johns Hopkins Surgeon*
and Author of Unaccountable

"Brilliant, and not just the thoughts—every detail. It goes down smoothly, the ideas unfold superbly, and the way Mastors teaches ideas that might be familiar to health observers is fresh and newly compelling. This could be the book that changes things."

—"e-Patient" **Dave deBronkart**, *Co-Founder,*
Society for Participatory Medicine, International Keynote Speaker

"I couldn't put this book down. Anyone planning to run a hospital should read this book first, and no one should go to the hospital without first reading it. It will save money and lives. It's an easy read, and has sensible and practical advice never before shared."

—Ilene Corina, *President, Founder, PULSE of New York,*
Community Outreach Director, Cautious Patient Foundation

"Had me hooked from the first page…chock-full of stories, vital information, checklists, links, and resources…a must-own for both clinicians and patients. You'll want a highlighter and notebook beside you."

—**Fred Lee**, *author,* If Disney Ran Your Hospital
9 1/2 Things You Would Do Differently

"Too little about health care is designed around meeting patients where they are at, [encouraging] patients and their caregivers to seek more and better information, rather than to suppress questions that might embarrass them. Mastors' *Design to Survive* offers a foundation for both providers and consumers to find the balance, and move to a world from provider-centered care to patient-centered care. If we re-shape the healthcare industry incorporating these simple concepts into everyday care, we will do one better: we'll have an informed patient and caregiver, poised to ask for the right care at the right time, and we will be aiming above patient-centered care, to empowered patient-directed care."

—**Stefan Gravenstein**, *MD, MPH, Professor of Medicine, Case Western Reserve University, Cleveland, Ohio, Adjunct Professor of Medicine and Health Services Policy and Practice, Brown University*

"Pat Mastors' voice shines brilliantly throughout this book. Rarely have I read a book focused on patient safety that is this engaging. Her visual storytelling combined with a spot-on explanation of how the IKEA business philosophy can change the delivery of healthcare inspires hope that positive change is possible."

—**Regina Holliday**, *International Keynote Speaker, Founding Artist, The Walking Gallery of Health Care*

"With the state of today's hospitals and nursing homes, no patient should check in without first reading this book. It is also a must-read for health care practitioners and designers."

—**Cynthia Leibrock**, *MA, ASID, Author,* Design Details for Health: Making the Most of Design's Healing Potential

"In our quest to create a more efficient, effective, and safe patient-centered healthcare system we need a pole star; we need examples, direction of other's tackling complex challenges in a way that is disruptive and transformative. Mastors' book encourages us, like IKEA, to be "quirky and imaginative" with our attempts to innovate healthcare. This is a fun read that will challenge and inspire."

—**Benjamin F. Miller**, *PsyD, University of Colorado School of Medicine Department of Family Medicine*

"…a stunning account of what [Mastors] and other patients and families go through…a gripping and essential read for consumers and health professionals, both practicing and teaching."

—**Patty Skolnik**, *Founder, Citizens for Patient Safety*

"Every Hospital Administrator, Every Nurse, and Every Doctor needs to read this book. More importantly, Every New Hospital Patient and those that love them need to ask their Hospital Team if they have read it and have a copy to hand out when they arrive—because if we do not demand change, it will never happen."

—**Alex Fair**, *CEO, Medstartr.com*

"If you or a family member need hospital care, this book offers a simple, easy-to-understand survival tool to help keep the unthinkable—a serious medical error—from turning into the irreversible."

—**Michael L. Millenson**, *author,* Demanding Medical Excellence: Doctors and Accountability in the Information Age

"Pat Mastors has come up with the model we need to improve care by using the IKEA model of partnership between provider and patient. Toxic hierarchy, obfuscation, lack of transparency and accountability, needless complexity and failure to implement proven standards have assured repeated failures in our current delivery system. Enough. This is the book all care providers should be reading on their first day of nursing or medical school."

—**Jean Rexford**, *Executive Director, Connecticut Center for Patient Safety*

DESIGN
TO
SURVIVE

9 WAYS AN IKEA APPROACH CAN
FIX HEALTH CARE & SAVE LIVES

PAT MASTORS

NEW YORK

DESIGN TO SURVIVE
9 WAYS AN IKEA APPROACH CAN FIX HEALTH CARE & SAVE LIVES

ISBN 978-1-61448-433-2 paperback
ISBN 978-1-61448-434-9 eBook
Library of Congress Control Number: 2012952888

Morgan James Publishing
The Entrepreneurial Publisher
5 Penn Plaza, 23rd Floor,
New York City, New York 10001
(212) 655-5470 office • (516) 908-4496 fax
www.MorganJamesPublishing.com

Cover design by:
Michael Graves with Dounia Tamri-Loeper

Photography by:
Salvatore P. Forgione.

Foreword drawing by:
Michael Graves

Other drawings by:
Pat Mastors

Interior Design by:
Bonnie Bushman
bonnie@caboodlegraphics.com

In an effort to support local communities, raise awareness and funds, Morgan James Publishing donates a percentage of all book sales for the life of each book to Habitat for Humanity Peninsula and Greater Williamsburg.

Get involved today, visit
www.MorganJamesBuilds.com.

Habitat
for Humanity®
Peninsula and
Greater Williamsburg
Building Partner

This book is dedicated to every person—in white coat and wing tips, or jeans and sneakers—who finds joy in bringing comfort and healing to another.

Apprehension, uncertainty, waiting, expectation, fear of surprise, do a patient more harm than any exertion.
—Florence Nightingale

It irritates me to be told how things have always been done. I defy the tyranny of precedent. I cannot afford the luxury of a closed mind.
—Clara Barton

Table of Contents

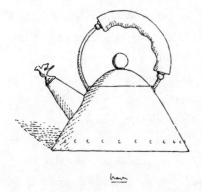

Foreword

By Michael Graves

When Pat Mastors interviewed me for this illuminating book, I immediately knew that I had met a kindred spirit. My own story—of sudden paralysis resulting from a sinus infection, and the ensuing frustrations of surgery and rehabilitation—is not unlike the many gripping stories that she uses to illustrate the state of health care in America. These personal accounts catch our attention and reveal the sometimes-shocking reality of health care systems, methods, and facilities that are unnecessarily complicated or flawed. Alongside these accounts of patients and their families, Mastors introduces a wealth of studies and statistics and succinctly frames the problems. The lack of simple common sense is a constant theme, a theme that resonated with me both as a patient and as a designer.

I am an architect with a design practice that ranges from buildings and interiors to furniture, consumer products, and graphic design. I have spent the past nine-and-a-half years paralyzed from the chest down and am mobile only by wheelchair. Despite paralysis, I thankfully did not lose the ability to use my mind and my hands. I therefore have been able to continue my life's work, becoming more and more committed to the health care aspects of what we do. We have recently designed houses for Wounded Warriors with myriad disabilities, we are working with health care companies on patient-centered care facilities, we are designing products that range from acute-care patient room furniture to aids for daily living, and we have created signage that even those with low vision can read.

What we have learned is that there is a tendency in health care design to overcomplicate things and not think holistically. For example, when Stryker Medical asked us to design an over-bed table and bedside stand for a hospital patient room, we discovered that the prevailing tendency in the marketplace was to add more functions and features to each piece, to outdo the competition. We, on the other hand, asked ourselves, "Can a piece of furniture help control the spread of infection?" The answer is yes. Our approach was to simplify the pieces, make them more functional by removing features, make them safer by making them lighter and easier to clean, and empower patients and caregivers by making them intuitive to use. This small example is analogous to Mastors' vision on how to improve health care delivery and outcomes as she moves across the entire spectrum of the health care field, topic by topic, with IKEA as her guide.

It was a stroke of genius to apply the IKEA model to health care, since this forward-looking company revolutionized home furnishings by creating an efficient partnership between retailer and customer in a smart, cost-effective manner, by design. For me, good design speaks to functionality as well as appearance. I often admire the simplicity of IKEA furniture and how it is straightforward and even intuitive to assemble and use. And it appeals to a wide audience. All of those attributes are what we should expect in a healthcare system, as Mastors explains. Mastors identifies nine ways that the IKEA model can be applied, from making us feel welcome to developing a simple, comprehensible cost structure. Her presentation is as clear as the logic of her ideas to improve health care. What Pat Mastors says is simple, straightforward, easy to understand and implement, and not expensive. Her lists of do's and don'ts are simple and direct. They reflect a deep understanding of the issues, reinforced by research. Her passionate plea for simplicity and common sense deserves notice. There's so much good advice here that I have made this book mandatory reading for our design staff. And for a patient, the book's advice might just save your life.

Michael Graves is a world-renowned architect and designer credited with raising public interest in good design as essential to the quality of everyday life. He designs sophisticated buildings and complexes worldwide, though Americans may best know his landmark Disney properties, such as the Swan and Dolphin hotels. Graves' designs of household objects include the iconic Alessi whistling bird teakettle and more than 2,000 products for Target stores and others. He's received thirteen honorary doctorates and many prestigious awards, including the 1999 National Medal of Arts and the 2001 Gold Medal from the American Institute of Architects. In 2011, the Center for Health Design named him one of the top 25 most influential people in healthcare design. He taught architecture at Princeton University for nearly forty years, and in February 2013 was appointed by the Obama administration to serve on what's widely known as the Access Board, bringing his singular aesthetic and insight to the world of accessible design.

Preface

Simplicity saves lives.

The body thumped gently against the side of the pool.

I lowered myself for a closer look, checking for a twitch, a gasp, any sign of life. Legs splayed out stiffly from a bloated belly. The eyes, I saw, were dull and lifeless.

Grimacing, I fished the mouse out by the tip of its tail, sorry that again, I was too late. Grimly I walked it to the fence and tossed it over, into the thick woods that surround my house. Some random fox, at least, would benefit.

We'd put in a swimming pool for the kids. Every morning I'd scan the surface and then lift the skimmer cover, braced to discover what hapless new creature had come here for a drink, only to get sucked into something much bigger than it bargained for.

For me, this was a problem. I am one of those crazy ladies who stops traffic to shepherd turtles and ducklings across the road. When my daughter found a baby hummingbird with a broken wing, I laid it on a bed of grass clippings and drove it to the wildlife clinic (sadly they could not save it). And now, the deaths of these animals in my pool weighed on me. Imagining their final, desperate struggles, I knew I had to do something.

I squatted down to surface level (or eye level, for a furry little thing paddling desperately for a way out) and took a good look at the world from a mouse-eye view. No nook or cranny offered a foothold. Even the steps were under five inches of water. But it gave me an idea. I scrounged in my garage and found the lid from a Styrofoam cooler. I poked a hole in the corner, threaded a piece of string through the hole, and tied it to the pool ladder. Anchored to the edge of the pool, floating on the surface, maybe it would provide those struggling animals with a way out.

The next morning, when I lifted the skimmer cover and peered inside, nothing peered back. It was the same for the rest of the summer, and it's worked remarkably well every summer since. With a small change to the physical landscape, the pool had stopped being a death trap.

Bottom line: give it a simple tool, and even a rodent with a brain the size of a jellybean will work like hell to save itself.

As hospital patients, how easily we become that hapless mouse. We find ourselves in an environment that, to outward appearances, is life sustaining, but which can quickly grip us in a confusing and frustrating battle for survival. We're isolated from all that's familiar and known, uncertain which direction is the right one. And the more we struggle, the longer we're "in," the weaker we get, and the greater the risk we'll never get out. And sadly, the "system" too often spends countless hours and dollars studying and refining the pool design, filling system, fence construction and local wildlife habits, when a 50-cent piece of Styrofoam could help solve the problem.

The chance of being killed in a hospital per patient day is greater than the chance of being killed during the height of battle during the war in Iraq per soldier per day. According to the Centers for Disease Control (CDC), more Americans are killed in hospitals every year (99,000 from hospital-acquired infections alone) than during all the years of the Vietnam War (58,000).[1] A government study in November 2011 concluded that 1 in 4 Medicare patients suffers some kind of harm in the hospital, and that 500 Medicare beneficiaries are killed *every day of the year*.[2]

Did you know that a checked bag on an airline flight is still exponentially safer than a patient in an American hospital? It is not very comforting to consider that a toothbrush has a better chance of reaching its destination than a patient has of leaving a hospital unscathed. This begs the question…why?… The primary reason it's so tough to change the system is that no less than the culture of medical practice has been challenged and is, in effect, resisting change. This is cultural inertia, the "this is the way we've always done it" syndrome, yet the root cause of poor patient safety performance lies squarely in the mythology that human perfection in medicine is achievable—the presumption that humans can practice without mistakes.

—**John Nance**, aviation and health care consultant
*Why Patients Should Fly: The Ultimate Flight
Plan to Patient Safety and Quality Care*

"As doctors, we swear to do no harm," says Marty Makary, MD, a Johns Hopkins surgeon and author of *Unaccountable: What Hospitals Won't Tell You and How Transparency Can Revolutionize Health Care*. "But on the job we soon absorb another unspoken rule: to overlook the mistakes of our colleagues. The problem is vast. U.S. surgeons operate on the wrong body part as often as 40 times a week. Roughly a quarter of all hospitalized patients will be harmed by a medical error of some kind … The human toll aside, medical errors cost the U.S. health-care system tens of billions a year. Some 20% to 30% of all medications, tests and procedures are unnecessary, according to research done by medical specialists, surveying their own fields. What other industry misses the mark this often?"[3]

Brent James MD, Chief Quality Officer at the Intermountain Healthcare, says we need to look at all this in a different way. "Don't compare it [medical harm] to domestic airline travel; you should instead compare it to flying combat, under fire," he says. "Anything that is powerful enough to heal can also harm. As a direct result, you're usually walking a very thin line between help and harm, and it is effectively impossible to avoid sometimes stepping across it. In other words, if you lose the injuries you could also lose the benefits, and the benefits massively outweigh the harms."[4]

These benefits—lives saved and bodies healed, against often discouraging odds—leave us awed and grateful. But it's hard to feel comforted when more people in the United States die of medical harm than anything else except heart disease, diabetes, and cancer.[5]

Several years ago, all of this hit home. My father entered the hospital for surgery following an accident at home, and died there six months later, from complications of an illness he didn't have at the time he entered the hospital. Even as a medical reporter, I'd had no idea how common this experience is. I've since learned a lot about the infection that killed my father, and it's plenty scary (more on that later).

It's scarier still that even the best doctors in the best hospitals can't stop harm from happening to their own. Not even the likes of Donald Berwick, MD, founder of the Institute for Healthcare Improvement, a nonprofit organization driving quality improvement around the world. Berwick learned this firsthand after his wife Ann developed symptoms of a rare spinal-cord problem at a leading hospital. As reported in *Time* magazine:

> *…His concern was not just how she was treated; it was that so little of what happened to her was unusual. Despite his best efforts, tests were repeated unnecessarily, data were misread, information was misplaced. Things weren't just slipping through the cracks: the cracks were so big, there was no solid ground…[For example] an attending neurologist said one drug should be started immediately, that "time is of the essence." That was on a Thursday morning at 10 a.m. The first dose was given sixty hours later, on Saturday night at 10 p.m. "Nothing I could do, nothing I did, nothing I could think of made any difference," Berwick said in a speech to colleagues. "It nearly drove me mad…No day passed—not one—without a medication error." If that could happen to a doctor's wife in a top hospital, he says, "I wonder more than ever what the average must be like. The errors were not rare. They were the norm."*
>
> —Q: What Scares Doctors? A: Being a Patient," *Time*, April 26, 2006

Why does this happen?

Today's nursing and medical staff are under the gun—for performance, outcomes, reporting, and improving the patient experience—even as they grapple with staffing shortages and long hours that put patients at risk. They're juggling a multitude of complex tasks, any one of which can be the turning point toward healing or harm. A sudden cardiac arrest down the hall, or a device not being available when it's needed, can throw the strictest safety routine and most skilled professional off-kilter. Shift changes, where the care of patients is "handed off" to new staff, are notoriously risky times for error. Says Berwick, "A patient with anything but the simplest needs is traversing a very complicated system across many handoffs and locations and players. And as the machine gets more complicated, there are more ways it can break."[6]

Add to the mix that all people make mistakes, but in the culture of medicine physicians aren't supposed to talk about theirs. So they can't learn from them. Another issue: a small number of doctors are just plain "bad apples", something you find in every profession, but dangerous in a field where people die and colleagues are squeamish about calling each other out. (In *Unaccountable*, Marty Makary describes a doctor privately referred to by colleagues as "HODAD", which stands for "Hands of Death and Destruction".) In chapter 7 we'll look at how bad doctors and the myth of practicing with perfection contribute to medical harm.

But the most widely shared view of what causes medical harm, as Berwick alluded to, is that it's practically built in to the system. Says Brent James: "the vast majority [is] from *system* failures—predictable problems that arise when human beings interact within complex systems using dangerous tools."[7]

If true, it begs the question: when something is predictable, can't it be fixed?

To appreciate what we're up against, let's go back to the aviation analogy, and imagine you're the medical cockpit crew "flying" patients toward safety in the hospital: no two planes (patients) are alike; no two cockpits (exam rooms, operating rooms) have the instrument panel arrayed in exactly the same way. Destinations, weather patterns and fuel levels shift constantly, and a random, life-or-death crisis can emerge at any moment. Supplies may be there when you need them, or maybe they won't. Cost factors play a role:

the airline might pressure you to fly the plane a certain way or to a certain destination because that's how they'll make more money. The "passengers" might decide not to do what you ask them to; they won't sit with seat belt buckled and won't keep their bags out of the aisles. Some of them bang on the cockpit door, wanting more peanuts. Each passenger has special needs, but their seat assignment may change several times, so sometimes you can lose track of who needs what. Every day, new research is published on how to do a better job flying planes, only you're too busy flying planes to read it. If all that isn't bad enough, the system is structured so you and the entire flight crew and the air traffic controllers will hand over the plane to a new crew every few hours, and you must communicate effectively and accurately to the new team all the variables you've been dealing with, as well as your playbook of how to proceed. All this, while keeping the plane flying smoothly and on course. Oh, and you'd better make sure all the passengers not only land safely, but had a great experience.

Meantime, passengers in our "health care flight" are not offered a 90-second demonstration before takeoff of how to save themselves if and when something goes wrong. They're not given life rafts and oxygen masks. If they notice and report the equivalent of smoke coming out of an engine, it's often met with pushback, arising from a paternalistic culture where they're supposed to sit there and do what they're told. When the worst does happen, there is no burning wreckage, no charred Teddy bear offering visible, irrefutable evidence of catastrophe. There is no black box recorder. TV crews do not camp out on the patient's (or family's) doorstep waiting with breathless anticipation for an eyewitness account that will be broadcast ad nauseam over a 24-hour news cycle. (Without the airline's advertising dollars, the media themselves would have trouble surviving.) Congress does not demand answers and accountability.

Is it any wonder mistakes keep happening? Is it not obvious we need all hands on deck to tackle "predictable problems that arise when human beings interact within complex systems using dangerous tools"?

The only way to drive improvement in this tangled thicket of variables, risks and agendas is to have a system aligned around one goal, and make everything work toward it. I suggest that goal should be doing what's best for patients. In this ideal world, providers and systems would respond to feedback with the singular focus of a stockbroker watching a ticker. Whenever patient safety or engagement faltered, they'd aggressively seek solutions, reducing the complex to the simple, and eliminating any variable that could cause harm. They'd communicate with pictograms and instructions anyone could understand. They'd be open and truthful about the risks, admitting they don't know everything and can't be everywhere.

And they'd ask patients for their help and partnership. Like the IKEA furniture company, the entire model of health care would be predicated on *engaging patients to participate*.

That's the essential premise of this book. The golden nugget that's been largely missing from all the hand-wringing about fixing health care is facing how urgently patients need to join the team.

IKEA is the largest furniture retailer in the world and a global powerhouse. Built atop a mountain of flat-pack "serve yourself, build it yourself" furniture, its model offers huge lessons on how simplicity, quality, affordability, and *customer engagement*, can achieve success across scores of countries and in dozens of languages. The bargain with customers is posted on the walls of IKEA showrooms, from Abu Dhabi to Zlicin (Prague): "You do your part. We do our part. Together we save money."

You may not even realize you're also attracted by what's called "The IKEA effect". It's defined as a love of things we help create. (It's not just our own babies we think are perfect.) In a Harvard Business Review article, "The IKEA Effect: When Labor Leads to Love", marketing professor Michael I. Norton writes, "...Labor enhances affection for its results. When people construct products themselves, from bookshelves to Build-a-Bears, they come to overvalue their... creations."[8]

Could we foster this pride of accomplishment in building our own health care outcomes?

What would an IKEA approach look like in health care? It might start with laser-like focus on meeting "customers'" where they are with language and literacy, not where we wish they would be. It might build a systematic approach to accommodating their varying abilities and desires to engage. It might ask if patients and their advocates, like the mouse in the swimming pool, would be better off if their environments supported a clear path to personal initiative and recovery. It might supply them with a few simple but critical tools to succeed. It might find patients made more practical choices when the cost of care was transparent. And above all, it might engage patients to "co-create" good outcomes, rather than expecting them to continue in their historic role as passive recipients of care.

Says Atul Gawande, MD, a surgeon who writes about quality in health care, "I think the most important part the patient plays is not being passive about their part on the team. We [physicians] are not great at drawing out the patient; we've wanted the patient to be passive and not so involved, just do what we say…I think what we're learning is, the patients play a key role." [9] Adds Diane Pinakiewicz, former president of the National Patient Safety Foundation, "Healthcare is an entire industry that was built around a passive customer who didn't think he or she had the right to question anything."[10]

That's beginning to change, partly through a current wave of health care quality improvement initiatives (you'll read about them here), and partly because the patient activism movement is finding its feet. But it's not working fast enough. Like my father, many people will continue to enter hospitals with no clue that medical harm is so common, or in many cases, preventable. In this book we'll get a layman's tour of this complex and bewildering landscape, pointing out the pitfalls to avoid, as well as the "islands of excellence" that prove better to be attainable. In the unforgettable personal stories of patient advocate friends and colleagues, and the honest insights of top medical providers, you might see a way to avoid your own medical Waterloo. During those times when you can't, you'll see how you can be part of the culture change that begins with awareness.

Admittedly, IKEA has a ton of advantages over health care in creating an efficient, holistic, integrated delivery system. There are no complex life-or-death decisions emerging twenty-four hours a day. No aging infrastructures. No onerous regulations or governing body telling you what to do. No barrage of professional journals, new techniques, and conferences to keep up with. No customers demanding furniture without a penny to pay for it. No labor unions. No lobbyists trying to steer your actions for personal gains. And no infectious diseases that, if left unchecked, could some day wipe out your entire client base. Also, as a private company still essentially in the control of its founder (now run by his three sons),[11] IKEA is also as close to a kingdom as you can get: management is autonomous, nimble, and accountable only to a small, family-based cadre of insiders.

No one's suggesting building a BILLY Bookcase is tantamount to replacing a knee, or that patients should bear responsibility for ensuring their own safety. The science and delivery of patient care will always lie squarely in the hands of those who treat us. As we saw in Don Berwick's case, even the most educated and well-connected patient in a high-performing hospital isn't immune to medical harm. But to continue with our paternalistic, "top-down" culture of health care is to dismiss all that patients can bring to the table. Surely we can do better than that.

We are born designed to survive. Think of how quickly a cut heals, a liver regenerates, or the metabolic system kicks in to save a child that falls through the ice. The will to live can drive survivors of a plane crash to eat the flesh of the dead, or a hiker trapped by a fallen boulder to amputate his own arm. Yet in the hospital, when professionals are caring for us, we put our survival instincts on hold. We don't swim for "the Styrofoam platform". In part, because we are sick, stressed and overwhelmed; but also because we're confident others will save us. And the "others" are also so confident they can save us, or the system so chaotic, there is often no Styrofoam platform offered.

From the waiting room to the operating room to the boardroom, *we patients* have the most skin in the game. We'd do well to step up and protect it.

We can begin by scouring the landscape to discover "affordable solutions for better living". Yes, that happens to be the IKEA motto. But in the pages ahead we'll borrow it, and hold it up as a metaphor for all that health care could be…if we wanted better for our children.

Introduction:
My Story

Late one night in August of 2005, my father, Bob Stegeman, got up to use the bathroom, tripped and fell down the stairs. Several days later, a persistent pain in his neck sent him to the emergency room, where an X-ray confirmed a fractured vertebra in a sensitive position in his spinal cord. It was something of a miracle, we learned, that my dad could actually walk around and function. He was immediately admitted to the hospital for surgery.

For years I'd been a news and medical reporter at a local TV station, and I had faith in the folks at this hospital. As Dad's only daughter, I also wanted to keep a close eye on his care.

My father greeted me that first day of his hospital admission in good spirits. Thank God the gravity of his neck injury had been discovered in time. The surgery would be delicate, but he was in the hands of an excellent surgeon. He could probably go home after a week's recovery.

Except—he had a low-grade fever. Before surgery could take place, he'd need to spend a few days on antibiotics. (As I'd later learn, this week on antibiotics was likely part of a "perfect storm" of conditions that would determine what ended up happening to him). When Dad was finally wheeled into the operating room, the surgery to fuse his neck vertebrae went well. But while he was still recovering in the ICU, I noticed his abdomen under the sheet was distended and hard. I alerted his medical team.

The next day, in the step-down ICU, Dad had a procedure to ease the pressure on his intestines. But soon after, he was talking to my mother when he suddenly went cold and clammy, his speech trailing off. Alarmed, she alerted the nurses, and my father was whisked back into the operating room. His intestines had ruptured. The surgical team would need to clean out as much of the spilled contents as possible, cut out the ruptured portion of his bowel, and attach a colostomy bag. Already weakened from the previous surgery, his chances of survival were about fifty-fifty.

I sat helpless by my father's bedside, watching as a dozen IV lines snaked fluids and drugs into his body, helping him fight sepsis and shock. A team of nurses tended lines, checked IV bags, and adjusted machines. Behind the breathing tube taped to his mouth and the oxygen tube in his nose, my father's face was so bloated it was almost unrecognizable.

My mind went to so many things…how excited I was as a little girl when he'd come home from work—I'd throw my arms around him, breathing in the smell of his aftershave…spotting him in the audience at my ballet performances, tears in his eyes…his endless patience as he coached me to drive the stick shift on the wheezy little Fiat he couldn't afford but bought me anyway…how he'd pull out his clunky camcorder whenever he visited, capturing everything that moved—the kids riding their rocking horse, or the dogs strolling across the lawn…the times people who worked with Dad would approach me in the grocery store or parking lot, and tell me how proud he was of his daughter on TV.

We asked his surgeon and the rest of the medical team what had caused Dad's colon to burst. They said they just didn't know. My brothers arranged to fly into town, having been told it might be time to say goodbye.

But amazingly, and despite the guarded prognosis of his doctors, Dad eventually opened his eyes. Days later the breathing tube came out, and he began to talk again. I took it as a good sign when he started complaining about the hospital food.

But between two major surgeries and long days on a respirator, my father had become weak as a kitten. He couldn't stand or walk. He could barely hear, since water had spilled on his hearing aids during his first days in the hospital. We posted notes around his room, reminding caregivers to speak up when they talked to him. But this proved fruitless, as his caregivers rotated constantly, and his room was switched a dozen times—sometimes due to an infection he'd contracted, sometimes for staff convenience. He coped stoically with an outbreak of a painful skin rash diagnosed as shingles (an effect from the chicken-pox virus that emerges under stress). When his health finally stabilized, his six foot-one frame had dwindled from 175 to 137 pounds.

The gift of this time with my father was that I came to understand more about him, and the life that had molded him. Dad was a Korean War veteran, the son of an immigrant watchmaker from the Netherlands and the first in his family to graduate college. He'd been a top executive at a catalog mail-order company for most of my childhood, but had struggled a bit since the year it had folded, back when I was a young teenager. Both he and Mom had stepped up and taken jobs to pay the mortgage, support us four kids and send us through college. As a child of the Depression and fiercely independent, Dad had never carried credit card debt, never borrowed money (our students loans being the exception) and never asked for help. It you'd asked, I would have said he was stubborn and thrifty. His independence was a mark of pride, I see now. Except for his family of which he was wildly proud, that independence was probably the most defining thing about him. That's why it was so hard, during the weeks and months he was the hospital, to watch him lose it.

How do you describe a life withering away well before that last breath is taken? Dad had not asked for much out of his retirement: attending his grandchildren's baseball games and tennis matches; puttering in his little garden, mowing the lawn, cooking up a batch of shrimp scampi or Chinese spare ribs, and reading about cars, science and nature. He would drop everything to pick up a grandchild from soccer practice or run an errand for us. He had a soft spot for animals and doted on his cat, Sasha (who would let only him pet her). He was also fiercely private, emotionally and physically. During my lifetime, even as Dad would fan himself in 90-degree weather, we'd tease him about the fact he'd never wear shorts. I'd never once seen him without socks and shoes. We don't think about our parents' quirks in real time, but looking back, I realize it really mattered to him—for whatever reason—to be that private about his body.

What's it like to lose all privacy and control? To watch your body become less and less your own? To go for weeks on end being told when, how and what to eat? To yearn for the luxury of walking outside, going to the bathroom alone, or sleeping through the night undisturbed? What does it do to your spirit when the feel, sight and smell of catheters, colostomies, and urine bottles dominate your physical space day after day? Knowing I had to brace myself every day just to enter his room, what was it like to *live* there?

Dad, however, had trust in the system. He would follow the rules and do what he was told. He said he could put up with anything to get back to his life.

Because he had infections, Dad was essentially a one-man "hazardous zone." A sign outside his door alerted all who entered to "Use Contact Precautions". It was posted next to a cart stacked high with folded paper or cloth gowns, and boxes of disposable gloves. I "suited up" before entering his room; upon exiting, I'd peel off the gown and gloves and toss them in a bin nearby. This process was designed to limit the spread of whatever bacteria Dad had tested positive for. Often it was MRSA (a type of staph infection); a few times it was *C. diff* (I'd never heard of it, but the nurses said it was very common). At that point, to me these were just odd-sounding names for something I couldn't see and that didn't seem particularly debilitating, relative to all my father's other problems.

There was much I didn't know.

We all focused on Dad's getting well enough to go home. At that point it was still a realistic hope. But first he had to gain weight and be infection-free. Only then would they release him to the rehab hospital, so he could regain his strength. Dutifully, he drank cases of a calorie-rich nutritional drink. Meekly he obeyed his physical therapist's orders to cough, do leg lifts, and walk.

In October, two months after Dad first entered the hospital, I read a news story about germs in hospitals. According to research by Dr. Chuck Gerba, a microbiology professor at the University of Arizona, "TV remotes in hospitals tend to convey more harmful microbes than toilet-bowl handles, bathroom doors, or call buttons."[12] Gerba detected, on average, 320 different types of bacteria on TV remotes, compared to an average 91 in the rooms in general. Sites tested included handrails, call buttons, tray tables, all doorknobs, faucet handles, and flush handles.

I lifted my eyes from the newspaper and looked at my Dad, who was dozing in his hospital bed. I spotted the TV remote (which was also the call button) resting near his hand. The device was never in the same place twice. It ended up falling off the pillow or tucked under his covers, and I'd seen it drop on the floor a few times. Also, virtually everybody that came into the room handled it.

Of course it would be dirty. With all those little buttons and delicate electronics, it would be tough to clean (though I hadn't seen anyone cleaning the remote or his bed rails or the doorknobs, come to think of it).

I filed the thought away. We finally got Dad into rehab, and then home. Ultimately we had two weeks to move my parents out of their house of more than forty years and into a hastily purchased, handicapped-accessible condo.

It was an intense and emotional time, but we were elated when Dad, shuffling along uncertainly on his walker, came home for Thanksgiving. He was also with us for two family birthdays and for Christmas. It seemed like the worst might be behind us.

But his colostomy was causing him a lot of trouble. In January he reentered the hospital for surgery to reverse it—to reinsert the intestine into his abdomen and reconnect it.

The surgery went well. But on February 12, 2006, six months after his fall down the stairs, the nurse looking in on him at 2 a.m. found him unconscious, his vital signs barely registering. Doctors said they suspected he'd "aspirated [swallowed] something into his lungs and choked."

My husband drove me through swirling snow to the hospital. *Just yesterday, he was talking about his hope to drive a car again. After all he's been through, surely Dad will beat this, too.* I clung to the thought.

I found my father again hooked up to multiple IVs and machines, his body and face bloated. His care team had waited for me to arrive before inserting the breathing tube. I pressed Dad's hand and told him I was here. Did he see me? Or know I was there? I honestly can't be sure.

My mother and older brother arrived. Shortly after, the surgeon who'd performed both of Dad's abdominal surgeries battled his way in through the storm. He told us he wanted to re-open the surgical site, to check for leaks or anything he could fix. But he emerged from the ICU just a short time later to sadly tell us there was nothing he could find—and nothing he could do. "What happened?" we asked. He said he just didn't know.

We reached my other brothers on the phone. It was surreal to hear the words coming out of my mouth. We went back in the room. The machines around him continued to hiss and beep, but the spirit of my father was gone. I held his hand and said goodbye. I remember sobbing wildly as the rhythm of the machines slowed…and went silent.

We buried my father. After fifty-two years of marriage, Mom was a widow. We began adjusting to being a family of five instead of six. I wrote a letter to the president of the hospital commending the wonderful staff that had cared for my father and fought for him on his final day.

But it didn't make sense. Dad was only seventy-six, and had never gotten sick a day in his life. What had happened to him? How could a surgery and hospitalization expected to take ten days end like this?

What I've learned since then, about the world of hospitals and the prevalence of infections and medical errors, is something everyone should know about. Hindsight and research offer an idea of how easily medical harm can occur—even in the finest hospitals.

In real time, it was a while before we started trying to put things together. According to my father's death certificate, his cause of death was "sepsis," which is "the body's response to an overwhelming infection." But how could that happen virtually overnight?

As with many families, the frustration of having no answers led to talk of a lawsuit. Among my family, the conversation was brief. I wanted no part in it, for several reasons. I never felt my father had poor care. Most everyone had been attentive and, from what I'd seen, had done the best they could. I also could not imagine long months of depositions and antagonism, prolonging the darkness of an event that had drained our family for months.

But I *did* want answers. Per the hospital's process, I faxed a request to receive my father's medical records. (I never did get a response; but I did eventually get answers.) Meantime I wanted to put my energies into something positive and forward thinking.

I remembered those germy hospital TV remote controls. Maybe I could purchase some covers and donate them to our hospital. At least that would be a step toward fixing the patient's environment, cutting down the germs that had given my father infections. I scoured the Internet, looking for disposable covers, but couldn't find anything. That surprised me, since you see those see-through covers everywhere on tools and instruments in doctors' and dentists' offices . Wouldn't hospitals want to eliminate a major potential vector of infection?

It seemed like someone should make one. One day in my kitchen, I grabbed some plastic bags, tape, and an X-acto knife and put together a prototype. Through a friend at the hospital, I got in to see the infection-control people. I shared my idea and asked if they'd try some covers out, if I got some made and donated them to try out. They listened politely and said they'd get back to me. The response came indirectly months later: "It's not mandated by CDC guidelines," and "There's no way to measure whether it's effective."

I gave the prototype to a contact that deals directly with hospitals around the country. Maybe someone would embrace the idea. But when he got back to me months later, the response wasn't encouraging. "Hospitals don't want to add the expense."

We were looking at spending pennies, potentially saving several more days in the hospital and thousands of dollars per patient.[13] I was getting some new insights into what I was up against.

While awaiting this feedback, I was digging deeper into research on germs in hospital rooms. When I stumbled across hospitalinfection.org, what I read there nearly took my breath away.

The following is paraphrased from the website. Betsy McCaughey, the former Lieutenant Governor of New York, runs the site.

Infections in hospitals kill 99,000 people each year—more than AIDS, car accidents, and breast cancer combined. That's like a jetliner crashing each day, killing nearly 300 people. For decades, no one has been charged with inspecting hospitals for cleanliness, or mandating that they be cleaned at all. Though restaurants and cruise ships are subjected to these inspections, hospitals, even operating rooms, have been exempt.[14]

Boston University researchers who examined 49 operating rooms found that more than half of the objects that should have been disinfected were overlooked. A study of patient rooms in 20 hospitals in Connecticut, Massachusetts, and Washington, DC, found that more than half the surfaces that should have been cleaned for new patients were left dirty. Lab coats, doctors' neckties…studies show both carry harmful bacteria that can be transmitted from patient to patient. These items are rarely cleaned. At the University of Maryland, 65 percent of medical personnel confessed they change their lab coat less than once a week, though they know it's contaminated. Fifteen percent admitted they change it less than once a month. Superbugs such as staph can live on these polyester coats for up to 56 days. A 2006 study in the Journal of Hospital Infection showed that one-third of blood-pressure cuffs rolled from room to room carried C. diff spores on the inside of the cuff.

The CDC and other organizations urge caregivers to clean their hands between patients, and even advise patients to speak up and request that caregivers have clean hands. Yet hand-hygiene compliance by health care workers in many facilities hovers around 50 percent. And as long as hospitals are inadequately cleaned, doctors' and nurses' hands will be re-contaminated seconds after they're washed—when they touch a medical chart, open a supply closet, pull open a privacy curtain, or contact other bacteria-laden surfaces.

I was appalled, as a relatively well-read reporter, that I'd had no idea things were this bad. And as I talked with medical contacts from my reporting years, I finally learned the truth from one of them: my father had died of complications from a *Clostridium difficile (C. diff)* infection. Suddenly, all the pieces fit into place. Everything that had happened now made sense.

A Stealth Killer

If the way this disease maims and kills people sounds like a horror story— it's because it is.

The *C. diff* bacteria, I read, occur naturally in the intestines of a small percentage of people. But in the hospital or nursing home, there's a substantial risk you'll pick it up and ingest it (eat it) by touching something contaminated by a previous patient (like a dirty bed rail, or the hands or clothing of caregivers who've touched infected patients), then touching your mouth or nose.[15]

C. diff in the intestine (the organism has also been found recently in healthy farm animals, especially piglets and calves) tends to live in balance and harmony with other bacteria. A healthy person might never have a symptom. But when your immune system is weakened (such as when you're in the hospital), and you take certain antibiotics (as my father did during his first week in the hospital), the "good" bacteria in your gut get killed off. This is *C. diff's* opportunity to thrive and begin releasing these toxins into the gut. This soupy toxin leads to violent diarrhea, dehydration, and intense intestinal cramping and dysfunction. It can lead to "toxic megacolon," where gases literally build up so much that the colon bursts. When that happens, the contents of the intestines spill into the abdominal cavity. When bacteria from the ruptured intestines enter the bloodstream, it can lead to what doctors call septic shock, a "gross insult" to the body, which is often fatal. (That my father survived this initial event is a testament to the immediacy of his surgery, his physical strength, and the quality of his care.)

Another concern is how *C. diff* "pays it forward" by infecting the next patients. With apologies for being indelicate, the violent diarrhea from a bad *C. diff* infection can spatter and spill all over the place—on bedpans, furniture, toilet seats, linens, telephones, stethoscopes, fingernails, rings, floors, infants' rooms, remote controls, and diaper pails. The millions of C. diff spores contained in this spatter are incredibly hardy. They can live for months on surfaces, ready to infect another patient through hand-to-mouth contact. (C. diff bacteria have been found in the aerosol ejected from a flushed toilet nearly two feet above the rim, and most hospital toilets have no lid to close…good reason not to leave your toothbrush exposed).

I wonder…did my father come into the hospital with *C. diff* already in his body? Or, while on his course of antibiotics, did he touch a contaminated phone or IV pole, and then touch his mouth or nose? (People typically touch their face one thousand times a day.) We'll never know. But my father had dentures, and he had no way to clean his hands before eating, even if he'd known how important hand hygiene was. In any case, why on earth didn't we know *anything* about it? And what of the patients who were in the rooms after my father left them? Did they contract *C. diff* infections?

What I later learned is that a new and virulent strain of *C. diff* showed up about a decade ago in U.S. hospitals, four times more lethal than the previous strain. It releases toxins into the colon at a rate 16 to 23 times greater, and is also resistant to antibiotics. (I also learned C. diff can become chronic; my father's continuing symptoms, and his eventual death from sepsis, are part of a devastating disease process much better understood today than it was at the time.)

The more I read about hospital-acquired infections (and there are many bacteria besides *C. diff* that cause infections)—which can attack an IV site, wound, intestines, bloodstream, urinary tract, lungs, or other organs—the more I felt other patients and families needed to know about them.

I launched an informational website and heard from many families who'd also lost loved ones to infection in the hospital. I contacted my state representative and with Rep. Eileen Naughton's help, got an infection-reporting law introduced in our legislature (so that the death of my father and others would actually be counted). Many of us testified before committees of the Rhode Island House and Senate. Together we flooded committee members' in-boxes with e-mails urging them to pass the measure. (They said they'd never before had so much e-mail in support of a bill.) The governor signed the legislation in 2008.

The state health department director invited me to serve on our hospital-acquired infection reporting advisory committee (where I serve to this day). I asked a hospital colleague if we could work on handing out information to patients when they entered the hospital. She told me "patients' health literacy was too low, and there were different languages involved." So I again approached Rep. Naughton, who introduced a second patient safety measure. This one would require that patients be informed in writing and upon admission (or as close to admission as possible) about the risk of infection, and behaviors that can keep them safe.

Then-eighteen-year-old Emily Croke was among those who testified. An only child, she was about to graduate from high school when her father went into the hospital for treatment of esophageal cancer:

...At the time of his surgery, the threat of infections was never discussed. Initially after his surgery, he was fine, and I was able to speak with him. Within forty-eight hours of his initial entry into the hospital, we were told things were not looking good, and he might not make it. Come to find out, this reaction was due to infections he acquired within the hospital.

Over a six-week period, my father caught several infections, including C. diff, MRSA [methicillin-resistant Staphylococcus aureas, a type of staph infection], and Pseudomonas...there were also so many absolutely repulsive things that I witnessed while my father was in the hospital that not only caused the spread of these diseases, but should not have even occurred under any circumstance. For example, while fighting C. diff, which resides in the colon, the hospital staff gave him an enema. When my mom later walked into the room, there were feces all over the floor, which no one bothered to clean up. My mom ended up cleaning the floor, which not only presented a threat to her and to other sick patients, but also to every visitor and staff.

During the early hours of August 25, 2008, I sat with my family by my father's bedside as we watched him take his final breaths. No one ever would have expected six weeks earlier that this surgery would result in death, due to factors completely unrelated to why he was having his procedure. My mother is forty-three and is a widow. Every day, I have to struggle with the memory of watching my father die and seeing the pain that my loved ones have had to bear...[16]

This second measure also passed. As of today, more than two years later, our work continues to implement its provisions.

I'd discovered the limitations of a legislative approach. I'd also learned from attending the annual conference of the Association of Professionals in Infection Control (APIC) in 2008 that hospitals were overwhelmed with trying to curb the problem, and that no easy solutions promised improvement any time soon. Knowing that every day, people continued to enter the hospital completely unaware of the risks, I kept thinking— *patients need tools and a "heads-up". Right at the bedside.* In the back of my mind was the TV remote cover. With a card tucked inside, it could also convey critical information to patients.

I took a deep breath and tapped a bit of money I'd put aside. I found a company to manufacture the remote covers, and with my husband's support and blessing, went "all in" to put together an "Infection Defense Kit" that a patient could take with them to the hospital. In it went remote covers, hand sanitizer, blood-pressure cuff barriers, a disinfectant spray, wipes (including bleach wipes), and an informational booklet. With high hopes, I launched the kit at a news conference and invited speakers. The director of our state health department spoke about the threat from hospital-acquired infections. Joe Amaral, MD, the former CEO of the hospital where my father died (and a big supporter), advised that "patients could no longer afford to be the passive recipients of care." The local AARP director urged that patients and families be more proactive. A friend spoke tearfully about losing his father to a *C. diff* infection.

I hoped the kit would at least be a conversation starter—a point of engagement—between patients and providers, helping them work together.

The kit reached patients in fourteen states and in Canada, mostly people already well aware of the risk of infection in the hospital. But it soon became clear just how naïve I'd been. First, while some hospital staff welcomed patients being proactive (and several actually used kits for themselves), the message that patients should protect themselves from harm was not one that hospitals exactly embraced. Most did not return my phone calls and emails. As for consumers, I'd built a solution to a problem most people didn't know they had and apparently didn't think would ever happen to them. (We advocates say that talking about medical harm to someone who hadn't experienced an adverse event is like describing being kidnapped by aliens.) I had a mission as big as the sky, but no alliances, no distribution plan, and no marketing budget to accomplish it.

I entered a local business-plan competition looking for ideas and support. The judges praised my goals and saw the need, but they did not select my company. They said, "You have no IP ["intellectual property"; something unique and proprietary]. No business will invest in you."

I gave the kits away to local senior citizens. But I was also "stubborn Dutch," like my father. I wasn't down yet.

The Mavens of the Patient Safety Movement

During this time, I also came to see I was far from unique in my advocacy for patients. After reading her story online during my research, one of the first people I reached out to was Helen Haskell, an early champion of the patient safety movement. For this distinction, she paid a terrible price. In 2000 her healthy, gifted 15-year-old son Lewis Blackman underwent elective surgery to correct a relatively common anomaly present at birth, known as sunken chest syndrome.

Lewis grew weaker in the hours after surgery. His heart rate climbed to 142 beats per minute (normal is 60 to 100), and his temperature dropped to 95 degrees. His eyes became hollow, his skin drained of color, and cold sweat poured off him. Helen was terrified, but it was the weekend, and the physician who performed the surgery was not available. Despite her repeated pleas, the staff dismissed Helen's concerns and refused to summon the surgeon or any other veteran doctor. As Monday morning dawned, thirty hours after surgery, Lewis went into cardiac arrest. Despite frantic, eleventh-hours efforts to save him, he died of blood loss and infection. The likely culprit: a too-strong dosage of the painkiller Toradol, which had eaten a hole in his stomach. In 2005, the *Lewis Blackman* Hospital Patient Safety Act became law in South Carolina and required among other things that all clinical staff in hospitals must wear identification tags, so their rank is clearly visible to patients and families. The hospital settled without a lawsuit, and Helen plowed part of the settlement money into founding the non-profit organization Mothers Against Medical Error (MAME). Since then she has devoted herself full-time to patient advocacy.

Says Helen today "As the years go by, I learn more and more how big a role weekend care plays in medical harm. I find that it is a factor in a shocking percentage of medical injuries, if you just ask. Most people are focused on other things and don't even realize that this entered into it." [17]

I'll always know how old Lewis would be, had he lived. He was born the same year as Nick, my oldest child.

It was Helen who recommended me, based on my work on patient safety legislation, to attend the 2009 conference held annually by the Consumer's Union (CU) Safe Patient Project (CU, which also publishes *Consumer Reports,* actually wrote the model bill adopted by many of the twenty-seven states that have passed infection-reporting laws, including Rhode Island's). Here, I met patient safety advocates from around the country. Hearing their stories for the first time filled me with sadness and outrage.

Patty Skolnik co-founded Citizens for Patient Safety after a nightmare that ended in the maiming and death of her only child. It began the day

Michael, a 22-year-old college student, passed out. The family physician, looking at test results of Michael's brain, said he did not need surgery. A neurosurgeon, however, offered a different opinion. "You're lucky he didn't die when he passed out. He needs surgery in the next forty-eight hours." The doctor said the cyst on Michael's brain was blocking his cerebral fluid and causing his brain to swell to life-threatening levels.

Patty checked out the profile of the neurosurgeon on the website of the Colorado Board of Medical Examiners. Nothing unusual came up, she says. "I Googled him and found only that he had his degree from where he said he did." What she did not and could not know was that this neurosurgeon was being sued for the death of another patient in Atlanta and had operated on the wrong disc.He had also operated on and disabled another patient in Atlanta.

(Though they choose not to name him, calling him only "the physician", Patty and David refused to sign a gag order—a legal pledge not to publicly discuss details—about what happened next.)

After his parents had left the hospital for the night, the neurosurgeon obtained a signature from a heavily-medicated Michael on a consent form to do brain surgery. When the Skolniks returned to the hospital the next morning, their son was already in the operating room. The procedure was supposed to take three hours. Michael was wheeled out six and a half hours later.

No cyst had been discovered. But it soon became apparent that six hours rooting around in Michael's brain had caused tremendous damage.

Michael lost the ability to walk, speak, eat, became partially blind, and was paralyzed except for spastic movement of his right arm and hand. Over months in the ICU he suffered from hallucinations, blood clots and a range of infections. He changed hospitals more than ten times and gained 100 pounds. He retained the mental capacity of a third grader, and most of his days were spent in pain and on heavy medication. He could move his right hand into a few gestures, indicating "a little," "a lot," thumbs up," "thumbs down," and "stop." Occasionally he would spastically form a gun with the same fingers and point it at his own head. On June 4, 2004, after opening his eyes and mouthing "I love you" to his parents, Michael died of massive organ failure, 32 months after the surgery.

The heartbroken Skolniks had vowed to Michael—who'd been pursuing a career as an emergency medical technician—that they would leave health care "better than he found it". And that's what they set out to do.

The realization that patients had no meaningful access to important information about their doctors propelled the Skolniks to change the law. They wanted to make sure that physicians' malpractice history would be available in a quick online search. The legislator who sponsored the bill, Morgan Carroll, says, "Patty met with every legislator and said, 'I'm a mom. I would like a meeting with you and to take a few minutes to show you a video.' The video was an excerpt about Michael's story from the 'Today Show'. One meeting at a time, she moved people, and began to grow our support." Patty found champions in the Colorado Medical Society, in the state's largest malpractice underwriter, and on both sides of the aisle. "Patty, with no legislative experience whatsoever, was able to get support for her idea at every turn," says Carroll. During a public ceremony, the governor signed The Michael Skolnik Medical Transparency Act in 2007. The Skolniks lobbied for two subsequent patient safety bills that also passed. Another is pending.

Patty now does advocacy training around the world. Among her clients is the U. S. Department of Defense. Seasoned war veterans hearing her story have been moved to tears.

At the 2010 annual meeting of the Consumer's Union Safe Patient Project, Patty had just that day received her first DVD copy of the documentary "From Tears to Transparency—The Story of Michael Skolnik."[18] We'd struck up a friendship at a previous conference, and she invited me to watch it privately with her.

Patty's warmth, approachability and strength are what make her such a successful voice for others. As we watched the film together, I could only begin to understand the price she has paid to do this work. Imagine reliving the horror of losing your only child in such an unthinkably painful way, played out before your eyes. I had no words. I rocked her and cried with her.

Meeting people like this can't help but change you. You realize the next person in that hospital bed could be your child. And you get an inkling of why patient advocates work so hard.

When the conference ended, Alicia Cole needed help getting through the airport, and I enjoyed the opportunity to get to know her better as I pushed her wheelchair through security. Alicia, founder of the Alliance for Safety Awareness for Patients (ASAP), is as warm and beautiful as she is strong and feisty. "Alicia the warrior" is what she called herself on her MySpace page—the one she set up after nearly dying of *necrotizing fasciitis* (flesh-eating disease). And 'warrior" is how I see her, because six years after nearly dying in the hospital, she's still fighting for justice and compensation from the medical system.

Alicia has been a working actress for years. She'd been a lifelong athlete and healthy enough to run the LA Marathon in 2001. Then in 2006 routine gynecological surgery led to an infection. It was Alicia's mother who first spotted a small dark spot near her daughter's incision. By the time she convinced the nurse to summon the doctor, an hour and a half had passed. In that time, the small dot had become the size of a quarter. The infection was spreading so quickly there was no time to waste: the physician, when he finally arrived, told Alicia's mother to "put on gloves and a mask…right then and there the doctor and my mother proceeded to open up my incision, extend it out by about 2 inches on each side, and began to squeeze out pus and drainage. It was the most surreal moment of my life."[19]

The infection continued to eat away at the tissue of Alicia's abdomen and nearly caused the amputation of her leg. Six surgeries followed, and for years Alicia lived with a gaping, oozing wound. (Like many advocates, Alicia is a fanatic about insisting on clean hands from everyone who touches her.) Now she speaks, lobbies, and inspires others to heighten awareness about patient safety. "I lived to tell the tale," she says. "And I *will* tell it, for every person who did not make it through."[20]

Through this network of new friends and colleagues, I also met Ilene Corina. Ilene founded PULSE (Persons United Limiting Sub-standards and Errors in health care) of New York after her three-year-old son Michael bled to death at home in her arms—the day after a "routine" tonsillectomy.

...Not a very religious person, I couldn't believe that there could possibly be a God that would cause this much pain. That my heart would be torn right out and I was supposed to have a reason to fight to survive the pain I felt. Why should I fight it? There was nothing left in life for me here...

Still in disbelief, I found a lawyer to help me search for answers about why Michael on that warm spring day, from a procedure that so many people get routinely, died. What did I do wrong? Did I do everything possible? Was I a good mother? Or did I fail my family— most importantly, the child whose life was entrusted to me?...

There was pain that the doctor, whom I trusted to care for the most precious thing in my life, now failed to return calls and tell me how this could happen. Now I began to want him punished, not for what he may have done, but for leaving me to sort this out and become [the] emotional mess that I had become. I actually liked this doctor and believe in my heart, to this day, that he too suffered. But I would never know because he stopped talking to me the day the autopsy report concluded that my son died from a tonsillectomy...[21]

I continue to learn so much from the patient advocate community. But one certainty emerged in these early days: even the collective efforts of "the best of the best" advocates, with their successful lobbying, laws, collaboration, and conferences, were not working fast enough to stem the tide of infection and medical harm.

The Overlooked "Pain Point"

In light of this frustrating lack of public awareness, I still might have forged ahead with my Infection Defense Kit, except for a critical design flaw I discovered when visiting patients who had one: I'd often enter a patient's room and find the whole kit, and everything in it, had been moved to the window shelf, or placed on a table that was out of reach. It's just the way it is in patients' rooms: everyone touches and moves your stuff. If a patient can't reach something, it can't help them. Though discouraging, this observation about the patient's world highlighted a huge, overlooked "pain point" that makes the patient's world frustrating and unsafe (straining to answer a ringing cell phone that's been moved out of reach, or having no safe place to put down hearing aids).

I went back to the drawing board, immersed myself in research, and sought insights at conferences, hospitals, and from patients and those who care for them. I met with hospital administrators who clearly had their own frustrations. ("If you could JUST HELP US NOT LOSE SO MANY HEARING AIDS AND DENTURES!" exclaimed one wrung-out hospital executive.) I connected with a registered nurse, now a hospital consultant, who'd purchased an Infection Defense Kit for herself when she was a hospital patient. Judy Hager's encouragement of my intent to modify the kit, and her unconditional offer of help, was a true blessing.

Over the next several months I approached two product-development companies for help with creating the solution I envisioned. They loved where I was going with the concept, but their process involved front-end research, modeling, and testing—all outside my budget. They wouldn't make a prototype without it. I finally found myself back at my kitchen table, cobbling together a prototype "Patient Pod" out of craft foam, vinyl, hot glue, balloon clips, and nylon cord.[22]

When I showed my prototype to Fuzion Design of Pawtucket, Rhode Island, they immediately got it—and got excited about it. They also presented an affordable path to bringing what I envisioned into reality.

We sat around the design table, brainstorming, while Fuzion President Joe Cacciola sketched. Having a team to help was electrifying!

We wanted a pouch attached to some kind of clip that would go on the bed rail. The pouch would be soft, instead of rigid, as patients already have enough sharp edges touching their skin. The clip had to work on every kind of bed rail, walker, and wheelchair. It had to self-level it so it wouldn't dump out the patient's things when the bed rail got raised or lowered. The clip had to go on and off with minimal hand strength, but be strong enough to hold a fair amount of weight. It would have to include hand-hygiene tools. A message clip, notepad, and pen would allow patients to take notes and communicate. (In my father's case, for instance, I would have written a message and posted it in the clip asking others to "Please speak up.") A family photo would make a patient feel connected, and maybe encourage caregivers to strike up a conversation.[23]

This stage was where the "IKEA" name started to come up. I'd say "let's put a line drawing in the front showing eyeglasses and cell phone and lip balm, like an IKEA drawing, so people know at a glance what kinds of things go inside." (Simple line drawings and "helping yourself" are hallmarks of IKEA design.) The design team understood it had to work for the well-educated adult, for someone with language or other problems, or even for a child…the design so entirely focused on the way people use it, that frustrations would be neutralized. (Read how to get many of these benefits without a Patient Pod in chapter 4).

I was also excited to finally have a go-to-place for patient handouts right at the bed rail. Whatever pamphlet, tips, or education was put there could help a patient and/or his advocate while health and recovery was most likely top of mind.

But what I loved best was to be to help a person like my father feel some control over his space, his things, and his comfort. Everything else might be taken away from him, but he would still feel connected to his world and his humanity.

We launched the Patient Pod in 2011, after trying it out in several hospitals nationwide. Of the hundreds of patients who used it, every one of them said they'd recommend it to their family and friends. The device's potential to change the dynamic of care is still unfolding. [24] But there's no dismissing the issues that underlie its creation.

"The End of Modern Medicine as We Know It"

There's more to worry about, fueling the urgency for collaboration between patients and providers. New "superbugs," which may prove to be more dangerous than MRSA and other common infections, are now on the rise. The reason? They're resistant to *all antibiotics*.

Imagine getting an infection and being told, "There's absolutely no antibiotic we have to treat this." Things as common as strep throat or a scratch on your child's elbow could once again kill. Margaret Chan, Director-General of the World Health Organization (WHO), says it's coming. She warned in early 2012 that bacteria are starting to become so resistant to common antibiotics that it could bring about "the end of modern medicine as we know it." As a result, she claims, "Every antibiotic ever developed is at risk of becoming useless, making once-routine operations impossible. This would include many of the breakthrough drugs developed to treat tuberculosis, malaria, bacterial infections, and HIV/AIDS, as well as simple treatments for cuts."[25] (For a fascinating look at these growing dangers, read Maryn McKenna's book *Superbug: The Fatal Menace of MRSA*.)

More danger signs appear every day. For example in January 2013, it was reported that known treatments for gonorrhea, a sexually transmitted disease that can lead to pregnancy complications and infertility, are becoming ineffective. The last class of antibiotics, called cephalosporins, is weakening against gonorrhea infections worldwide (other classes of antibiotics had already lost their effectiveness). A report in the Journal of the American Medical Association says this drug resistance has now reached North America in sizable numbers.[26]

Part of the problem is over prescribing. The CDC estimates that half of antibiotics in the United States are inappropriately prescribed. They are frequently given out, often under patient pressure, to tackle colds and other viral infections where they do no good. Travel and immigration spread the resulting resistant bacteria around the globe.

A new WHO publication entitled *The Evolving Threat of Antimicrobial Resistance* also says antibiotics fed to farm animals play an important role. As Dr. Chan says, "Worldwide we use more antibiotics in healthy animals than in unhealthy humans." In the United States, about 80 percent of the antibiotics used on farms have routinely been placed in feed, to preempt possible infections rather than treating them when they occur (absent illness, more animals "fatten up").[27] The WHO has now appealed to governments across the world to support research into the antimicrobial resistance.[28]

In hospitals, a "post-antibiotics world" is already here. Superbugs like antibiotic-resistant forms of *Pseudomonas aeruginosa*[29] and *Klebsiella*[30] belong to a group called "gram-negative bacteria" (this refers to the way they stain when tested in labs). They are particularly dangerous and deadly because in some cases they are *completely* resistant to all current treatments. Says Dr. Brad Spellberg, Infection Specialist at Harbor UCLA Medical

Center, "...for gram-positives, we need better drugs; for gram-negatives, we need *any* drugs."[31]

As for *C. diff,* the disease that killed my father, an April 2012 government report says though screening and prevention programs in recent years have actually reduced certain hospital-acquired infections in some settings, *"Clostridium difficile (C. diff)* infection rates remain at historic highs... killing 14,000 Americans each year and adding an estimated $1 billion in extra costs to the health care system."[32] A USA Today investigation published in August 2012 puts the number of deaths at 30,000—more than twice the government report.[33]

C.diff is also moving beyond the elderly, now affecting hospitalized children,[34] birthing mothers,[35] and those in the community outside of medical institution[36]—wherever a patient's immune system is weak. And as mentioned earlier, if you survive an attack, *C. diff* can recur and become chronic, diminishing your health, well being, and lifestyle:

> *It has been over five years since I contracted C. diff during my hospital stay. I was in the hospital for the birth of our child, and as our parting gift, along with the formula we left on the bedside, I was also taking home a potentially fatal intestinal bacteria. We had a seven-day-old baby that I had to rip off my breast and put down every twenty minutes as I ran to the bathroom. My abdomen was healing from the major surgery one week earlier, and now this. I was too sick to be furious. I was mostly sad. It wasn't supposed to be this way.*
>
> *What was most shocking was learning how rampant this infection is, how common it is, and how inept the medical system is at dealing with it, tracking it, or giving people warning about it. Remember in school when there was a lice outbreak, or chicken pox, or scabies? The teachers sent home a note to the parents detailing the situation, explaining the symptoms, and telling people what to look for and what to do if they noticed their child having any of the listed symptoms. They were informed.*
>
> *Every person admitted to a hospital should receive a notice explaining the presence of C. diff on surfaces, and tell them what to look for and who to contact if they begin to have symptoms. The*

INSTANT someone is given Clindamycin, C. diff should be discussed as a probable collateral effect. No one at the hospital ever knew that I had contracted C. diff. By this alone I know that the numbers being reported are dramatically low. The lack of information provided by the hospital when the outcome is borderline predictable is egregious.

—**Amy Burke**, Doctor of Chiropractic,
as told to PeggyFoundation.org, 2012

All Hands on Deck

C. diff infection, and the battle to control it, offers an example of a problem that needs an "all hands on deck" approach. It's not just public awareness that's missing. Knowledge among physicians of how to treat *C. diff* is often lacking. Ironically a common practice, prescribing antibiotics to knock down a flare-up of symptoms, can set in motion a continuous cycle of relapse. (In chapter 8 we'll look at innovative and holistic ways *C. diff* has been successfully treated.) Another problem: few cleaners can kill *C. diff* in spore form, left behind on things patients touch. Bleach solution is the product of choice for hard surfaces (though there's evidence hydrogen peroxide is more effective).[37]

Hospitals control *C. diff* by monitoring patients on antibiotics, isolating patients with symptoms in private rooms, using contact precautions including gloves, and cleaning surfaces with bleach solution. Unfortunately, private rooms aren't always available, gloves and hand washing aren't always used faithfully, thoroughly cleaning patients' rooms is time consuming, bleach is corrosive to surfaces, and its fumes cause breathing problems for some cleaning personnel and health care workers. So you begin to see what we're up against in fighting this disease—and why it makes so much sense for caregivers to partner with patients on preventing *C. diff* infection in the first place.[38]

Some hospitals have successfully reduced *C. diff* infection rates by religious adherence to proven hygiene practices: The Jewish Hospital-Mercy Health in Cincinnati, for example, launched a high-priority initiative in 2009 to bring down its skyrocketing C. diff rate. By putting better controls on antibiotic use, better room-cleaning strategies and revamping care standards, the hospital dramatically cut its *C. diff* infection rate. In just six months, the average number of cases dropped from about 16 a month to fewer than half that number. "We weren't inventing anything new with this project—it was based on science, it was based on evidence, on best practices," says Azalea Wedig, the hospital's infection control specialist. "We didn't think we'd see such drastic results in six months." And the decline continues: From January through March 2012, the infection rate was down nearly 80 percent since the initiative began.[39]

But even as progress emerges, so do signs of how far we have to go. An NBC investigative report broadcast in February 2012, for instance, shows that too often, surgical tools are leaving the sterilization process still contaminated with hidden blood, tissue, and other debris from previous surgeries. Research published in April 2012 by the American Journal for Infection Control reveals 92 percent of hospital privacy curtains were contaminated with potentially dangerous bacteria such as MRSA and VRE (Vancomycin-resistant *Enterococcus,* a bacteria transmitted by fecal matter) within one week of being laundered. Between May 2012 and January 2013, the CDC reported fungal meningitis from a tainted batch of steroid shots traced to a Massachusetts compounding lab had struck almost 664 people victims in 19 states and claimed 40 lives—one of the most serious healthcare-associated infection outbreaks in U.S. history.

Until recently, there was little incentive—financially at least—for hospitals to prevent patient harm. If a patient got an infection after surgery, or fell out of bed and broke a hip, the cost of the extra care was tacked on to the insurance bill. But with new Medicare policies, those days—theoretically at least—are gone. Medicare no longer reimburses for a diagnosis you didn't enter the hospital with, including certain kinds of infections, bedsores, and injuries from patient falls—so-called "never events."[40] The federal government has also committed $10 billion over the next ten years to the new Center for Medicare and Medicaid Innovation, to test new approaches and models of care and payment that will improve services.

This support for innovation at the highest levels represents a sea change from the status quo, which has been to study ad nauseam just how bad the situation is. Don Berwick, former administrator of the Centers for Medicare & Medicaid Services (CMS) director[41], describes this with a saying he learned while working in the African country of Ghana: "You don't make a pig fatter by weighing the pig. You do so by changing the way you've been taking care of the farm."

Don Berwick is a visionary and a hero to patients and providers alike. But with all due respect: are we patients like pigs, awaiting whatever fate the farm (even a better farm) holds for us? Shouldn't we patients do more than root around in our little corner of the barn, passively waiting for someone to improve the farm?

The answer is yes, and not just to save our own respective skin. The future health of the entire system needs our partnership, for several reasons.

1. **We patients are a great resource.** Nearly ten years ago Charles Safran, MD, of Beth Israel Deaconess and Harvard Medical School, testified to the House Ways and Means Subcommittee on Health back in June 2004, "I want to note especially the importance of the resource that is most often underutilized in our information systems—*our patients.*"

    How can we patients help make health care better? To start, we can follow the lead of people like author, speaker, and blogger Dave deBronkart (aka e-Patient Dave).[42] Dave survived stage-four kidney cancer—not just because he had the best doctors or the best care (which he did), but also because he was engaged in the process every step of the way. His message: when you're facing a medical crisis, you (and your tribe of people) become a committed and powerful team of researchers on your particular situation. You might learn something even your doctors don't know (see point 2 below). Dave advises we scour the Internet for information, find online communities for support and insights, and (with humility and grace) share what we learn with our doctors—because, as Dave says, "there is no substitute for the trained mind."

2. **Docs can't keep up.** There's just too much new information in medicine emerging constantly to stay on top of it all—it's a virtual fire hose of new stuff pumping out at full throttle. Dr. Donald Lindberg, director of the National Library of Medicine, is quoted as saying, "If I read two journal articles every night, at the end of a year I'd be four hundred years behind."[43] As

deBronkart adds in his speeches, Lindberg confided to him years later, "Today, it's much worse." How is any physician, even the best in his or her field, supposed to keep up? It's just not possible. Instead of a physician feeling criticized or offended by a patient pointing out some new research, approach, or study, the good physician welcomes the addition of this information to his body of knowledge.

3. **It's in the dollars.** With the advent of value-based purchasing bundled payments, and accountable care (all of which reimburse providers for outcomes, not quantity of procedures), patient engagement has become a business imperative for providers. In short, providers will be paid more for happier, safer, more engaged patients.

Some hospitals are working to be ahead of the curve. Doors long closed to patients—in hospital boardrooms, policy meetings, and government committees—are opening (with some steady pushing by persistent patients and families). These pioneers are building trust and relationships with providers and other stakeholders. Such inroads are important and increasingly frequent events we patient advocates celebrate on the Facebook pages, message boards, blogs and Google Groups that connect the patient advocacy network. [44]

But trust—and true partnership—between providers and patients begins with *truth*.

In *Understanding Patient Safety*, Dr. Robert Wachter, Chief of Internal Medicine at the University of California, San Francisco writes, "When we step onto an airplane, we recognize that there is not much we can do to ensure our own safety—we simply trust that the airline and its employees have done everything they possibly can to keep us safe. A patient checking into a hospital or visiting clinic or surgery center should be able to enjoy the same level of trust."[45]

Wachter is right. But he's speaking of an ideal. For as long as the toothbrush in our checked luggage has a better chance of arriving safely at its destination than a patient has of emerging from a hospital stay unharmed, patients cannot afford to be passive travelers on their health care journey.

One Person's View

From the time I was a little kid, I craved answers. Long before Google, I would spend hours sitting on the floor in front of the bookcase in our house, pulling out volumes from Grolier's Encyclopedia, Popular Science and The Book of Knowledge. I'd surf them at random, fascinated for some reason to learn how General Grant beat General Lee, why there are no kangaroos in America, how the human eye sees color. I always thought, the more I know, the more the world will make sense. It's probably what propelled me into working as a news reporter. When my father's death diverted me to plunge deep into the workings of health care, it was like falling into a subterranean world I'd never known existed. My inborn curiosity and reporter's training left me no choice but to follow the leads wherever they took me.

I hope sharing what I learned will help you be smarter and more prepared than I was. "You wouldn't believe the number of patients who have told me their deciding factor in choosing a hospital was parking," says surgeon Makary of Johns Hopkins.

This has to change. The hope is by using the IKEA framework, we're breaking down the health care beast into relatable, digestible chunks. Then we can begin to chew on the countless opportunities to design our own medical choices.

It is the patient's time in history. *We* have to exert some "pull-through" if we want better, safer care, price transparency, shared-decision-making, and accountability from our providers. It means asking questions of our lawmakers and doctors, and holding them—and ourselves—accountable.

If we can achieve this common "value proposition", maybe we could build a better health care system together.

It's the way IKEA has been building success for seventy years.

1   If IKEA designed health care...

we would always feel welcome

Like any store, we hope our customers will want to come back. It is the role of customer service co-workers to encourage this, by...being tuned in to the customers' needs—before, during, and after a purchase...It's not only about being friendly and helpful to customers, but concerns store accessibility, rest and recreation areas, diaper-changing facilities, and call centers.

—from the IKEA website

IKEA is doing something right. Customers have made it the world's largest furniture retailer. Founded in 1943 by seventeen-year-old Ingvar Kamprad in Sweden, there are 338 stores in 40 countries (including 38 stores in the United States). In the fiscal year ending August 2012, 776 million visitors worldwide plunked down 27.5 billion euro ($36.4 billion US dollars). That's nearly enough money to hand a five-dollar bill to every man, woman, and child on earth. The company published 212 million catalogs in 29 languages—the most widely circulated publication in the world.[46] It's estimated up to one in ten Europeans is conceived in a bed made by the company. And in the UK, market analyst Mintel estimates that more than two-thirds of Brits visit IKEA more regularly than they go to church.[47]

Today, IKEA founder Ingvar Kamprad, nearly 88 at this writing, lets his three sons mostly run the place, but IKEA is still very much a reflection of his vision and values.[48] While other Swedish boys were reading comics, young Ingvar Kamprad pored over mail order catalogs. He began to sell matches and fish, and in 1943, at the age of seventeen, registered his own mail-order firm under the name IKEA—an acronym of his name and the farm (Elmtaryd) and parish (Agunnaryd) where he grew up. He started out selling pens, Christmas cards, and seeds from a shed on his family's farm in southern Sweden. In 1951, the first catalog appeared. He soon decided to concentrate on furniture, and an empire was launched.

Never been to an IKEA store? They're big-box stores, painted blue and yellow on the outside (the colors of the Swedish flag). Cavernous showrooms display furniture as though you're walking into someone's house—because they want you to feel at home.

When you enter, you pick up a pencil and paper, a map, a measuring tape, and a catalog (at some stores, a friendly greeter hands them to you). You can also grab a cart and an oversized bag for your purchases. If you forget any of this stuff—no worries. They're placed conveniently throughout the store. If you choose, you can drop off the kids at "Smaland", where they can watch a movie, color pictures, or play with toys. There's a secure check-in process, and parents get an armband and a pager. They'll alert you if little Johnny needs you sooner than expected.

Stroll along the designated path painted on the floor, displayed on the signage, and outlined in your map. You won't get lost, but it will take you past every corner of the store (there are shortcuts, shown on the map). Signs encourage you to linger over, touch, and try out each product, to flop on the chairs and stretch out on the sofas. Each item is clearly marked with a bold, black-on-white price tag. Want to buy it? Write down the aisle and bin number (also on the tag) on the paper grid provided. The wide-open spaces where customers stroll—nicely lit and filled with fully decorated rooms showcasing clever use of space—means no bumping your ankles around too-tight corners, and no worries about blocking the way for the shoppers behind you. Sit and linger at any time you choose. There's a colorful, hands-on kids' section, and a cafeteria selling food that's "tasty, uncomplicated and GOOD FOR YOU!"

> *Chat in our kitchens. Lie in our beds. Play with our elephants.*
> —from the IKEA website

Toward the end of the journey is an open-shelf "Market Hall" for smaller items. Then it's on to the "Self Serve" furniture warehouse to collect the stuff whose description and location you wrote down along the way (it's all stacked to the ceiling in flat-pack form). Finally, you maneuver your cart to a cash register and pay for it (no bags or bagging; it's do-it-yourself, but they'll sell you big cloth bags with their logo), and load your booty into or on top of your car (twine provided free in a dispenser). Once home, armed with simple tools and an instructional pamphlet, you build the furniture yourself. [49]

Why do people put up with going through what one anonymous blog comment called "a retail digestive tract"? Well, it's cheap! You can get an 18-piece FARGRIK dinnerware service for 6 for $24.99, a HELMER 6-drawer chest for $39.99, or an entire 108-square-foot kitchen with appliances for $3,119.

But IKEA did not build its empire on "cheap" alone. Its other company mantras are high quality and good design. That's how IKEA has become the darling of newlyweds, college students (and their parents), people living on a budget, and anyone who just likes its clean design lines, efficiency, and "green" sensitivity. [50]

Icons are always targets for potshots, and IKEA is no exception. One observation is that "IKEA" is Swedish for "particleboard," though comedienne Amy Poehler reportedly said it's Swedish for "argument" (because that's what assembling the furniture can lead to). Cartoons discovered on the web show an IKEA sign stuck in a field of new-fallen snow boasting "free snowmen," and an IKEA do-it-yourself leather couch that comes with two parts: a cow and a saw. Pranksters have offered up do-it-yourself assembly instructions online on how to make a HOUS, a BABI, or even a DILORIANN. Some of IKEA's Swedish product names have amusing or unfortunate connotations in other languages. The company has responded by quietly withdrawing them, including these products from English-speaking markets: the "Jerker" desk, "Fukta" plant spray, and "Fartfull" workbench.

IKEA fans are quirky and imaginative: there's a website called IKEAfans.com, unaffiliated with the company but devoted to, well, fans of IKEA, their questions and projects. Then there's IKEAhackers.net, a site connecting and showcasing the work of "hacks" who cobble together unique masterpieces from various furniture and product components. There's even the "Swedish Furniture Name Generator" at Blogadilla.com, where you enter your first name and it creates your Swedish furniture name. (I tried it; I am PATRYKA, a plain wooden dining chair.)

IKEA has evolved to be not just a company, but a culture:

Perhaps more than any other company in the world, IKEA has become a curator of people's lifestyles, if not their lives. At a time when consumers face so many choices for everything they buy, IKEA provides a one-stop sanctuary for coolness. It is a trusted safe zone that people can enter and immediately be part of a like-minded cost/design/environmentally-sensitive global tribe. There are other would-be curators around— Starbucks and Virgin do a good job—but IKEA does it best.

If the Swedish retailer has its way, you too will live in a BoKlok home and sleep in a Leksvik bed under a Brunskära quilt. (Beds are named for Norwegian cities; bedding after flowers and plants.) IKEA wants to supply the food in your fridge (it also sells the fridge) and the soap in your shower.

—Bloomberg BusinessWeek, November 2005

Kamprad describes the objectives for the Swedish furniture maker's "democratic design" as the trinity of *attractive form, inexpensive production,* and *high function.* That idea, combined with what Kamprad calls "the underdog's obsession with always doing the opposite of what others were doing," impelled him and his young, risk-taking associates along a path of constant innovation and experimentation.

Compare this mission to the "Triple Aim" of health care, as described by the Cambridge-based Institute for Healthcare Improvement (IHI), a leading voice in health care quality: "Improving the health of the population, enhancing the patient-care experience, and reducing the per capita cost of care." Interestingly, whether by accident or cosmic alignment, the goals of good health care have, at least on paper, a striking commonality with the goals of IKEA.

IHI: "The Triple Aim"	IKEA: "The Trinity"
Improve Health of the Population	High Function
Enhance the Patient-Care Experience	Attractive Form
Reduce the Per Capita Cost of Care	Inexpensive Production

IKEA stores, with their abundant, clearly marked customer parking; warm, inviting showrooms; smell of cinnamon buns baking as you enter; and attention to customers' needs throughout their visit project a feeling of welcome.

Hospitals vary widely in the ways their environments and staff project that "welcome feeling." However, too many have cheerless environments, poorly marked signage, and other traits that project an institutional, intimidating feel. The experience of David Goldhill, related in his article "How American Healthcare Killed My Father" will sound sadly familiar to many[51]:

Keeping Dad company in the hospital for five weeks had left me befuddled. How can a facility featuring state-of-the-art diagnostic equipment use less-sophisticated information technology than my local sushi bar? How can the ICU stress the importance of sterility when its trash is picked up once daily, and only after flowing onto the floor of a patient's room? Considering the importance of a patient's frame of mind to recovery, why are the rooms so cheerless and uncomfortable? In whose interest is the bizarre scheduling of hospital shifts, so that a five-week stay brings an endless string of new personnel assigned to a patient's care? Why, in other words, has this technologically advanced hospital missed out on the revolution in quality control and customer service that has swept all other consumer-facing industries in the past two generations?

Where true, there are many reasons for this, some relating to the notion that the insurance company, and not the patient, is the true customer of health care (more on that in chapter 6). But we'd be remiss not to point out that there are exceptional hospitals today that make the IKEA "welcome" pale in comparison.

The Dell Children's Medical Center of Central Texas, for instance, welcomes patients with healing, interactive artwork; a constellation of stars on the ceiling (and little telescopes along the railings); an aquarium; water elements; and no less than seven gardens, one of them spanning three acres and including a reflecting pond and bridge. Florida Hospital for Children in Orlando has a Disney partnership; Mickey and Donald Duck often drop in to visit. For adults and children, the Planetree organization insists on exacting standards for its hundreds of member hospitals. Its flagship hospital in Derby, Connecticut has a saltwater aquarium, music lounge, and a healing garden. Pediatric patients are whisked to procedures in bright red, cushioned Radio Flyers. (Planetree hospitals also empower patients by inviting them to read their own medical charts at any time and ask questions of their physician and nurse about what they read.)

More and more hospitals are offering valet parking, glass-and-granite lobbies, plush furnishings, upscale cafes, and for those who can afford it, much more. Singer Beyonce's VIP hospital suite, where she gave birth to baby Blue Ivy in January 2012, featured clubby furniture, a kitchenette, and flat-screen TV (actually four TVs; apparently she booked four suites together). Cedars-Sinai Medical Center in Los Angeles promises "the ultimate in pampering" in its $3,784 maternity suites. One wing in New

York Presbyterian/Weill Cornell has a penthouse wing with Frette bed linens, marble bathrooms, uniformed butlers, and elegant menu choices like hand-sliced smoked salmon with cucumber-yogurt-dill sauce, and filet of cod rollatini baked in lemon wine sauce.[52] Such lavish amenities are meant to attract top-paying patients (like the Saudi King who reportedly booked the entire fourteenth floor of the hospital in late 2011).[53]

But more often, hospitals face challenges in improving the "customer-facing" aspects of their institutions. Upgrades and staff cost money. Belt-tightening from non-reimbursed care and new regulations mean many hospitals are operating with the thinnest of profit margins. Some hospitals are stuck with aging infrastructures (anyone who's rehabbed an old house knows how pricey and tricky renovations can be). Buildings went up before the need for big parking lots, meaning a patient may have to park a great distance from the entrance, perhaps risk a parking ticket, and then wind their way through a confusing maze of offices, elevators, and corridors to get where they need to go.

Somewhere between the resort-like hospital offerings and the environment described by Goldhill is the "sweet spot" of democratic design: the hallmark of IKEA. Founder Kamprad describes the concept this way: "having a limited budget should not prevent people from creating a beautiful home, with practical and sensible furniture."

Beautiful, practical, and sensible are indeed possible, even in amenity-challenged, outdated hospitals.

It depends at least in part on your definition of what's beautiful.

I had my first baby in a timeworn urban hospital the year before a new facility opened its doors. The rooms were tiny, the floor cracked, and the lighting dim. But I had a healthy baby and wonderful, attentive nurses, and I couldn't have cared less what my room or the furniture looked like. Having a baby may be the best reason to be in the hospital, and in this experience I felt little of the anxiety of the truly sick. But I've spent long hours with several family members who've been through prolonged hospitalizations for life-threatening illness.[54] They will tell you that although a good medical outcome is tops, the nicest "stuff" is no substitute for a warm, caring staff, a kind word, a comforting smile, and a sensitive caregiver ensuring you have the privacy when you need it and a sympathetic ear when you're alone and scared. Attentiveness and concern for patients represents the "true beauty" of a hospital.

> *What makes a difference to the wounded and sick? Yes, good medicine is amazing science and phenomenal minds working hard to cure. However, let us not forget the small things: a warm smile, an ice chip, a warm blanket, a cool washcloth. A pillow flipped to the other side and a boost in bed. Holding a fragile hand while sitting by the bed of the dying in the deep recess of night. Jumping up onto a bed to do CPR… Staying alive, staying alive…Chapstick and a damp mouth swab. A patient comforted, a smile, a deep breath and heartbeat from someone resuscitated. This was a bit of my job over the last few days. We all do this. Every one of us. And this is not even in our job description.*
>
> —Respiratory therapist **Colleen Murphy Allen**
> *Posted online and used with her permission*

The story of Ken Schwartz, a lawyer working in health care, offers a case in point. Schwartz was forty years old and married with a young son when he got devastating news out of the blue: advanced lung cancer. He'd smoked an occasional cigarette in college and law school, but he had been living a smoke-free, healthy lifestyle since then. As he wrote in the *Boston Globe*, early on in the diagnosis and treatment process:

> *…the nurse was cool and brusque, as if I were just another faceless patient. But once the interview began, and I told her that I had just learned that I probably had advanced lung cancer, she softened, took my hand, and asked how I was doing. We talked about my two-year-old son, Ben, and she mentioned that her nephew was named Ben. By the end of our conversation, she was wiping tears from her eyes and saying that while she normally was not on the surgical floor, she would come see me before the surgery. Sure enough, the following day, while I was waiting to be wheeled into surgery, she came by, held my hand, and, with moist eyes, wished me luck…*
>
> *This small gesture was powerful; my apprehension gave way to a much-needed moment of calm. Looking back, I realize that in a*

high-volume setting, the high-pressure atmosphere tends to stifle a caregiver's inherent compassion and humanity. But the briefest pause in the frenetic pace can bring out the best in a caregiver, and do much for a terrified patient…I cannot emphasize enough how meaningful it was to me when caregivers revealed something about themselves that made a personal connection to my plight. It made me feel much less lonely. The rulebooks, I'm sure, frown on such intimate engagement between caregiver and patient. But maybe it's time to rewrite them.[55]

The very event that meant so much to Schwartz in this case— caregivers sharing a personal connection to his plight—flies in the face of what's advised in some medical schools. "I was taught to empathize with the patient; to talk about them, not about us" says Stefan Gravenstein MD, Professor of Medicine at Case Western Reserve University. "Imagine being taught NOT to do what perhaps comes naturally, in the quest of forming bonds with patients and their families?" Over the course of his career Gravenstein says he came to follow his own path, talking to patients and families "like fellow human beings". But the legacy of this training surely leaves its mark on the way in which many physicians interact with their patients…and begs the question: what are today's physicians-in-training being taught?

Ken Schwartz died of lung cancer less than a year after his diagnosis. But his legacy lives on in the foundation he started shortly before his death, the Schwartz Center for Compassionate Healthcare at Massachusetts General Hospital. Dedicated to strengthening the relationships between patients and caregivers, it also stands as a poignant testament to the power of the human touch, and human kindness, in affirming our basic humanity.

I've learned that people will forget what you said, people will forget what you did, but people will never forget how you made them feel.

—Maya Angelou

Painting a "Destination Postcard"

To honor patients' humanity is also to respect us as partners in our health care. Don Berwick, the former director of Medicare and Medicaid, challenged his colleagues during a speech to the National Health Services in 2008: "First, put the patient at the center—at the absolute center of your system of care...for everything that you do ... It is not focus groups or surveys or token representation. It is the active presence of patients, families, and communities in the design, management, assessment, and improvement of care itself ... it means equipping every patient for self-care as much as each wants. It means total transparency—broad daylight. It means that patients have their own medical records and that restricted visiting hours are eliminated. It means, 'Nothing about me without me.' It means that we who offer health care stop acting like hosts to patients and families, and start acting like guests in their lives."

Berwick's feelings about patients arise from the core of his being—from his experience at his own wife's bedside during a prolonged health crisis. Long before he painted this picture in 2008, some doctors were already providing it.

When Laura Esserman, a Harvard-trained breast cancer surgeon, joined the University of California at San Francisco in the early 1990s, radical mastectomies—surgically removing the breast, underlying chest muscle, and lymph nodes—were the norm. In addition, the process of getting a diagnosis and treatment plan was often brutally drawn-out and anxiety-filled...getting bumped from office to office, toting your records to different departments, referrals and delays in getting appointments. Then there was surgery, with follow-up radiation and chemotherapy treatments conducted at different sites and with different booking procedures and delays. Through the entire process, the woman wondered: "Will I live through this?" The anxiety-filled process appalled Esserman.

As related in Chip Heath and Dan Heath's book *Switch: How to Change Things When Change is Hard*, Esserman had a vision of how it might be different: a woman facing a possible breast cancer diagnosis could walk in at the beginning of the day, and by day's end, leave with either with the knowledge that the tumor was no problem, or with treatment plan in hand.

The big barrier to Esserman's plan was the lack of coordination among medical departments. If they could be integrated more tightly, in terms of their locations and scheduling, the patient would not have to leave the building and the experience would be built around the patient's needs, not the departments'.

As an associate professor at a large university medical center with little clout and few resources, Esserman's best assets were "her own tenacity and her ability to sell a vision of what breast cancer care should be"[56]. She and a colleague set up the Breast Care Center to operate for four hours, one day a week. With practice and persistence, they cajoled the medical departments to start working together in more integrated ways.

Eventually, the Breast Care Center achieved enough success that it was offered an entire floor in a new cancer center being built at UCSF. But Esserman was dismayed when she saw the proposed building layout: the radiology department would still be in the old building. Determined to achieve her "everything under one roof" vision for the patient, she gave up one-third of the Breast Care Center's new space to make way for a mammography unit. Patients flocked to the Breast Cancer Center. From 1997 to 2003, the number of patients seen per month jumped from 175 to 1,300.

The Center went on to become a major source of revenue for UCSF and a recognized national leader in breast cancer research. In essence, Esserman's simple, clear vision of "everything under one roof" for her patients was key to its success. As the Heath brothers say it in their book, Esserman "painted a destination postcard" and "sold the vision".

"What is good for our customers is also, in the long run, good for us." Those words could easily be a takeaway from Esserman's success at "putting the woman at the center of care". But in fact, those are the words of Ingvar Kamprad, founder of IKEA.

MAKING PATIENTS FEEL WELCOME:

Critical Opportunities for Health Care:

1. **In the waiting room, check in with patients whose wait has been twenty minutes or longer. Offer them an update, a forecast, and an option to come in at another time.** Emergencies do crop up,

patients show up late, and when it's our turn, we all want our doctor to take her time with us and answer our questions. We patients get that. What we want and often don't get is the same courtesy we'd extend to our manicurist or dog sitter: if at all possible, let us know you'll be late.

2. **No money for fancy lobbies? Build connections.** At least partly because future insurance reimbursements depend on them, hospitals are now paying more attention to "patient satisfaction scores", more formally known as Hospital Consumer Assessment of Healthcare Providers & Systems (HCAHPS) scores—those evaluations some of us are asked to fill out after we're discharged. The questions range from how clean your room was to how well the nurses and doctors attended to your needs. Of the questions that feed into patient satisfaction scores (and the "money" question: "Would you recommend this hospital to your family and friends?"), seven out of nine of the questions on these surveys relate to the empathy of caregivers.[57]

3. **Watch this TED Talk by physician and author Abraham Verghese on physicians and the power of human touch:** http://www.ted.com/talks/abraham_verghese_a_doctor_s_touch.html

Tips 4 through 9 borrow from Fred Lee's best-selling book *If Disney Ran Your Hospital: 9 ½ Things You Would Do Differently* (Second River Healthcare Press, 2004)

4. **Greet the patient by name and introduce yourself with a cheerful greeting.**
5. **Comment on anything special in the room, like flowers, pictures or cards.**
6. **Meet any other people in the room.**
7. **Ask if there's anything else they need or need explained.**
8. **Ask how they want the door left (open, closed, or in between).**
9. **Remember conversations to build on over the duration of the patient's stay.**

10. **Re-examine how you deploy caregivers.** Keeping the same caregivers assigned to the same patients for the duration of their stay enhances continuity, comfort, and potentially patient safety.

11. **Once a month, look around your office and waiting rooms for yellowed, peeling, dusty, dirty, and dead things, and remove them.** As humorist Erma Bombeck said, "never go to a doctor whose office plants have died". I've also walked by a row of hanging lab coats outside a hospital recovery room and been appalled at the stained pockets and dirty cuffs. In addition to the unhealthy germs they carry, the display makes me wonder what the rest of the hospital must be like.

Critical Opportunities for Patients & Families

1. **Know that beauty is only skin-deep.** Hospitals put their money into shiny new lobbies and gourmet meals because that's what patients often rate them on. Good, tasty food counts (and I believe it helps with recovery), but you can always bring in food from outside; not so with nursing care. Though a warm, inviting environment is healing, just be sure to put "beauty" in the context of quality of care in evaluating which hospital you'll choose. (More on researching hospitals online in chapter 3.)

2. **Reward hospitals and staff who make you feel welcome.** Write a letter to the hospital CEO and/or local newspaper. Give names and specifics. If your experience wasn't great, write the hospital about that too—constructively.

3. **Vote with your feet.** Know that you have choices. ZocDoc (ZocDoc.com) lets you search for doctors in your area by specialty, offers reviews and ratings, shows you available appointments, and lets you book an appointment through the website.

4. **Speak up!** Add your voice, literal or virtual, to the growing dialogue about the health care experience. Be part of something bigger.

2

If IKEA designed health care...

 # instructions would be understandable to a fifth grader

IKEA sells billion of dollars' worth of assembly-required furniture each year to consumers in 39 countries, in 27 languages. They've obviously figured out how to communicate successfully across diverse populations and cultures. How do they do it? IKEA assembly instructions use as few words as possible, with many pictures to illustrate how you put the parts together. Designers work at creating intuitive designs that try to make it obvious how the piece of furniture should be assembled. As author and risk management specialist Dr. David Hillson writes in his white paper "The IKEA Approach to Risk," "The goal is to make the task of self-assembly foolproof, so that anyone can construct the furniture correctly by following the simple instructions.

IKEA products are intended to work as well in Riyadh as they do in Reykjavík.

"House Perfect," *The New Yorker*, October 3, 2011

As we saw earlier, not everyone finds IKEA instructions simple or easy.[58] But few if any companies communicate written instructions across cultural, language, and lifestyle barriers as successfully as IKEA does.

In health care, payers and providers often do a poor job communicating with those they serve. Currently providers trot out "poor health literacy" as one reason it's fruitless to invest resources in engaging or educating patients (I've been told that myself). They are right about one thing: the way we do things now often misses the mark.

> *An elderly woman sent home from the hospital develops a life-threatening infection because she doesn't understand the warning signs listed in the discharge instructions. A man flummoxed by an intake form in a doctor's office reflexively writes 'no' to every question because he doesn't understand what is being asked. A young mother pours a drug that is supposed to be taken by mouth into her baby's ear, perforating the eardrum.[59]*

These examples, provided to *The Washington Post* by health care workers or patient advocates, illustrate a pervasive and under-recognized problem in the United States: America's alarmingly low levels of health literacy. About 36 percent of US adults have "basic" or "below basic" health-literacy skills.

According to the National Action Plan to Improve Health Literacy, "Two decades of research indicate that today's health information is presented in a way that isn't usable by most Americans. Nearly 9 out of 10 adults have difficulty using the everyday health information that is routinely available in our health care facilities, retail outlets, media, and communities."

Without clear information and an understanding of prevention and self-management of conditions, people are more likely to skip necessary medical tests. They also end up in the emergency room more often, and they have a hard time managing chronic diseases, such as diabetes or high blood pressure. Studies link poor health literacy, which disproportionately affects the elderly, the poor, and recent immigrants, to higher rates of hospital readmission, expensive and unnecessary complications, and even death.

The problem goes even deeper than that. According to the nonprofit Institute for Safe Medication Practices:

1. More than 40 percent of patients with chronic illnesses are functionally illiterate.

2. Almost a quarter of all adult Americans read at or below a fifth-grade level, while medical information leaflets are typically written at a tenth-grade reading level or above.

3. An estimated three out of four patients throw out the medication leaflet stapled to the prescription bag without reading it.

4. Only half of all patients take their medications as directed.

Furthermore, people who have difficulty reading or understanding health information are ashamed. They often hide the problem. In addition, low literacy isn't obvious. Researchers have reported poor reading skills in some of the most poised and articulate patients.[60]

This litany of failures not surprisingly adds up to higher costs. A 2007 study at the University of Connecticut says the cost to the US economy is as much as $238 billion a year.

Beginning October 2011, federal agencies under the Plain Writing Act began mandating the use of plain language in their materials. Though it's an encouraging development, there's a possibly naïve presumption that "uptake" by the patient will just happen; that because we write it differently, it will lead to behavior change. There are multiple reasons, cultural and psychological, that influence whether a patient will read, process, and follow these materials (that's if he doesn't toss out or lose them when he gets home, as with the medication leaflet stapled to the prescription bag). "You can lead a horse to water, but you can't make him drink" has become cliché for a reason. Overcoming this challenge points to a need for a "feedback" loop, where we confirm information is understood.

Another challenge—our global love affair with technology and the increasingly large role it is playing in health care reform—may also isolate some patients even further from the process of participating in their care. This may be especially likely among the elderly and the poor who currently account for a disproportionate percentage of health care costs.[61] For instance, my now eighty-two-year-old mother is not unlike many of her peers. She won't go near technology and though she has a cell phone, prefers to carry phone numbers and other critical information on hand-written notes in her wallet. Until such time as an IT solution is universal, used happily by everyone like her and running flawlessly, what kind of ownership of their health information can we give patients like her to ensure *she* can be the "constant" – the vessel of information continuity— between various care providers?

How about a two-way conversation? A process now gaining ground called "teach-back" does this, to great success: debriefing the patient as to what they understand and ensuring they have an action plan following discharge. The premise is akin to when we were school students: we resolve questions while we're in class with the teacher, so we can be successful later doing our homework.

Such a simple, low-tech teaching tool worked beautifully at the Mayo Clinic. From its website:

> *Though diabetes contributes to nearly a quarter million deaths in the United States annually, patients with chronic ailments don't always take their medication as prescribed. A Mayo Clinic research team has designed a simple tool to improve compliance with life-saving medications.*
>
> *Victor Montori, MD, an endocrinologist at Mayo Clinic and lead investigator of the study, recommends using this tool as a decision aid to spark conversation between doctors and patients about medication. It consists of an easy-to-follow guide with answers to four questions tailored to individual patients:*
>
> 1. *What is your risk of having a heart attack in ten years?*
> 2. *What are the benefits of taking statins as compared to not taking statins?*
> 3. *What side effects can you expect from statins?*
> 4. *What do you want to do now?*
>
> *"Conversations with patients about prescription medications tend to be brief and incomplete, but we found that when a decision aid was introduced, it was the start of a conversation in which the patient—*

now better equipped with information—felt empowered to participate in deciding whether a statin would be appropriate for them," Dr. Montori says.

Good Communication—An "Always" Event

Patient-focused events like teach-back, good hand hygiene, and making sure patients always know who is in charge of their care are gaining momentum as so-called "Always Events." (This is in contrast to "Never Events," such as infections and wrong-site surgeries, a label that's dominated the language of health care quality improvement). Stefan Gravenstein, MD, Clinical Director at Rhode Island–based Healthcentric Advisors, whose work with teach-back has won national attention,[62] says we can do teach-back better. "Even better than 'ask-back' would be if the patient or caregiver would *'write-back.'* In other words, write down what they think they are supposed to do, even if it is already printed for them." This would be akin to the student taking notes about homework while in class, to prompt his memory later.

Simple solutions exist to manage this process, including patient "binders" and the Patient Pod.[63 64] This patient-written "homework" ideally should stay accessible to the patient after discharge, says Gravenstein. "Not only can this information serve as direct reference for the patient; it's a resource for the nursing home, home health facility, or wherever she is recovering —a really time-efficient reporting mechanism to the various providers. It also gives the patient confidence to express what they're really doing, rather than what we think they're doing. And that makes us more effective in taking care of them."

Though electronic health records may one day render a paper copy of this material unnecessary, we have a long way to go before the process functions smoothly, and before technical literacy on the part of patients is sufficiently widespread for meaningful participation in this process. In the meantime, like a student without a backpack, managing the back-and-forth from hospital to nursing home, to home, and back again, means important papers, information, and personal items may easily be lost or misplaced. Without proper management of this material, there's a vast communication gap between what happens to you in the hospital, and what your doctor understands when you see her in her office. As written in the *New England Journal of Medicine:*

> Among the data that should always reach outpatient clinicians (your doctor in his office) are post discharge medication changes, follow-up plans and appointments, pending tests, and the details of advanced care planning—yet we know that such information is not always transmitted. For instance, we have found that about 41 percent of hospitalized patients have pending test results at the time of discharge, and often neither the discharging physician nor the primary care provider is informed about these test results.... These considerations are just the tip of the iceberg when it comes to the problem of ambulatory care (outpatient care) safety. [65]

The Institute for Safe Medication Practices puts it this way: Patient education requires a new approach—assume that everyone has a literacy problem. After all, people at all literacy levels prefer simple, straightforward instructions and written materials. Whether you're filling in a form or talking with a patient, here's what they say works:

Offer small amounts of information at a time. First, tell patients what they truly need to know to follow directions. Emphasize desired behavior, not the medical facts.

Provide written materials at a fifth-grade reading level or lower. Use clear captions, ample white space, and pictures, diagrams, or videotapes to help explain concepts. Most people, even those who read well, depend on visual clues to reinforce learning and spark memory.

Involve patients. Use focus groups of patients to help write personally relevant and culturally sensitive education materials. After they understand the information, ask patients how you should explain it to others.

Verify that the patient understands. Avoid asking yes/no questions and instead ask patients to show and tell you how they would take their medicine so that you can spot problems. (This is what teach-back is about.)

Keep your eye on evolving technology. For example, talking prescription labels (Talking Rx from Millennium Compliance or Envision's

ScripTalk), pill bottle caps connected through technology to our pharmacy to remind us to take our medicine (rxvitality.com), recording devices for prescription instructions (Asko Corporation's Aloud), and electronic pill organizers and reminders (e-pill, www.epill.com) are now being tested or are already on the market.

Companies like Polyglot Systems (pgsi.com) are also stepping in with technology solutions that improve communication across language and literacy barriers. Its ProLingua system, for example, enables hospital staff "to immediately speak over 7,000 common medical questions and directives in multiple languages."[66] It also provides customized medication and discharge instructions in a patient's primary language.

An unintended consequence of the technology wave in health care is what we're sacrificing to pay for it.[67] Some hospitals are cutting staff—the people who take the time to look patients in the eyes and communicate—to meet new federal standards for integrating technology. "You can hide behind technology and spend more time talking to your computer than to your patients," says Dr. Albert Wu, a professor of medicine at Johns Hopkins. "And as with any new thing, people screw things up worse before they make things better…Doctors say there is a temptation to trust computers too much: they seem objective and infallible, but if the wrong information is entered in the first place, or the bar-coded wristband is put on the wrong patient, it can be harder to prevent mistakes down the line. In one case study, a patient with pneumonia had his wristband mixed up with a diabetic patient and came very close to being given a fatal dose of insulin."[68]

There's an old saying: "Doctors are revenues; nurses are expenses." As resources are squeezed, who will answer the patient's call bell? Who will take the time to explain the procedure you're about to undergo? As housekeepers and aides are cut, who will wipe down the germs on your bed rails, change your bed linens, and wheel you to tests? None of these scenarios bode well for patient care.

Until those patients who consume the most health care resources are more engaged users of technology, our best hope to move us forward with patient engagement is to meet patients at their own level, to go where they are—not where we want them to be, or where it's convenient for them to be. That means literacy levels and technologies that embrace and do not intimidate them.

It's hard work. Think of the tremendous and relentless focus on the consumer experience embodied in Apple products. Said then-CEO Steve Jobs, "The goal is to design a product that so fits into the natural ways of life, how people customarily use things, rather than expect people to adapt—aiming to create a satisfying sense of the natural, intuitive, and simple."[69] The result: a phone or tablet so intuitive that lots of people who buy them never even touch the manual. It's that satisfying. And it builds a relationship of trust—a reputation—that brings customers returning again and again.

As a business like IKEA extends its reach around the globe, and the wider and more diverse its customer base becomes, the more critical it is that products, instructions, store layouts, websites, and everything it produces embody this consistency, simplicity, and intuitiveness. That should be top of mind for those designing health care products, handouts, hospital buildings, and even exam gowns—everything that touches patients.

MAKING INSTRUCTIONS UNDERSTANDABLE TO A FIFTH GRADER:

Critical Opportunities for Health Care

1. **Offer small amounts of information at a time.**
2. **Use language that is simple, clear and concrete** – the kind that could be understood by a 5th grader. Include visual aids wherever you can to explain concepts. If you're unsure whether or not a 5th grader would understand, go find one and ask him to point out which parts are confusing.
3. **Use focus groups of patients** to help write personally relevant and culturally sensitive education materials.
4. **Ask the patient to paraphrase what they understand** about their treatment plan to verify their understanding, instead of asking yes/ no questions. Ask patients to show and tell you how they would

take their medicine so that you can spot problems (i.e., teach-back).

5. **Don't let pursuit of technology distance you from "seeing" the patient.**

6. **Create a list of suggested resources** for where to find additional information (have a printout available)

Critical Opportunities for Patients & Families

1. **Be prepared to use your time with the doctor effectively.** Bring a notebook and write down questions you have as they occur to you. Be prepared to write down the answers when they come.

2. **Speak up and ask your questions!** Knowing what they are in advance will empower you against feeling intimidated. Knowing that you're part of something bigger may help you appreciate the power of your voice.

3. **When someone asks whether or not you understand**, paraphrase what you learned from the explanation instead of offering a yes/no.

3

If IKEA designed health care...

a one-stop website would help us learn, connect, and plan

Studies show that people cannot find the health information they seek on websites about 60 percent of the time. This percentage may be significantly higher for persons with limited literacy skills.

—Health.gov website, March 2012

Today's IKEA, like any forward-thinking business, has jumped firmly on the technology train, so consumers can maximize their engagement, purchases, and experience online. The interactive, award-winning IKEA websites (1.1 billion visits in 2012, or nearly three million each day) feature 11,000 products and allow you to shop for and design your room before you even set foot in the showroom. Online planners let you configure your kitchen or wardrobe, giving you a 3-D, rotating model of what it will look like, along with a printout you can take to the store. A virtual sales assistant called "Anna" will answer your online inquiries.

The *Web Globalization Report Card*, an annual benchmark of how effectively companies internationalize and localize their websites and applications for the world, has put IKEA on top for the last three years, saying it's "done an amazing job of balancing global consistency with local flexibility in every market it enters." In recent years IKEA opened its first stores in Latin America, Ireland, Bulgaria, and Bangkok. On deck for 2013: Lithuania, Serbia, and Zagreb.

Bottom line, IKEA does a great job integrating the customer's experience across both brick-and-mortar and online venues. That's marrying the best of "high touch" and "high tech," with neither embraced at the expense of the other.

This represents continual and relentless focus on how customers *use* not just the stores and products, but the website that guides the virtual shopping experience. Does the customer know where to go? Do they find the choices they want? Do they get frustrated and leave? What would make it easier? As in the showroom, the customer experience drives design.

Nowhere is this laser focus on how customers use things more important than in health care. It's not like there aren't plenty of websites and online communities serving up information about health facilities, providers, symptoms, a diagnosis, treatment options, or support groups. In fact, it's just the opposite; trying to gather information from the Internet can be like trying to take the proverbial sip of water out of a fire hydrant. (Just for fun, I Googled the phrase "one-stop website for health information" and got 385 million results.) Carolyn Clancy, MD, director of the Agency for Healthcare Research and Quality (AHRQ), estimated in March 2012 that there are more than 150 public websites offering data just on providers alone.

The US Department of Health and Human Services offers its "Hospital Compare" websites, which report some outcomes data on physicians, hospitals, and nursing homes (hospitalcompare.hhs.gov). However, these are not the easiest sites in the world to use. Even if you can figure out how to compare a few hospitals or physicians, the information is pretty vague e.g., "no different from the national average". What does this really mean? And is the national average for a given outcome a good benchmark?

Participants interviewed for a Commonwealth Fund study published in the March 2012 *Health Affairs* [70] said consumers also found data on many health care reporting websites hard to understand and use. The study identified six factors making public reporting and patient use of health care information difficult, if not impossible:

- Lack of consumer readiness and engagement
- Opposition from providers
- Lack of funding
- Political obstacles
- Insufficient data infrastructure
- Inadequacy of current measurement science

Hundreds of groups outside of health care offer databases for consumers, from the list of "America's Best Hospitals" published annually in *US News & World Report* to health care articles (and sometimes exposés) in *Consumer Reports,* to evaluations by patients (and others) on Angie's List.

How reliable is much of this information? That's all over the place. Some is rigorously risk-adjusted and scrutinized before it is released, some is raw and unexamined, and a great deal of it is shaded (or falsified) by those with a stake in the outcome. (Perhaps the most comprehensive source for hospital safety "report cards" is the Leapfrog Group, an independent, international nonprofit, based on research and public comment. In late November 2012, for the first time, the group identified "D" and "F" hospitals, which represent the most dangerous hospitals for patients in need of care. Go to hospitalsafetyscore.org.)

There's also the question of just how much consumers are using quality-reporting data. "The many earnest experiments at publishing quality data… attract miniscule numbers of consumer users, while Yelp is now in front of 60 million Americans every month looking for restaurant and dry cleaners' ratings. What do Yelp, Angie's List, and Urbanspoon know that CMS doesn't?" asks David Lansky, who drives quality improvement for a group of fifty medical institutions.[71]

So where does the consumer/patient look for information that's user-friendly, valuable, and trustworthy? Increasingly they're turning to another invaluable resource, made accessible by the Internet: their peers.

Says Susannah Fox of the Pew Internet & American Life Project:[72]

Just like peer-to-peer file sharing transformed the music industry by allowing people to share songs, peer-to-peer health care has the potential to transform the pursuit of health by allowing people to share what they know. It is the confluence of two powerful forces:

- *Our ancient instinct to seek and share advice about our health*
- *Our newfound ability to do so at Internet speed and at Internet scale.*

Peer-to-peer health care acknowledges that patients and caregivers know things—about themselves, about each other, about treatments—and they want to share what they know to help other people. Technology helps to surface and organize that knowledge to make it useful for as many people as possible.

In a subsequent blog post, Fox points out roadblocks to the path ahead:

- *The Internet also provides access to misinformation (which can sow distrust of online health information).*
- *Anxious people can make themselves even more anxious by reading about dire consequences of certain treatments, worst-case scenarios, etc. (the person [who raised this concern] laid out his observation that people with poor outcomes are the ones who continue to blog about a disease or injury, not the ones who are managing it well or who have gotten over it).*

As a health care consumer, you'll need to filter what you read online as you would for any other service or product, such as a car, a vacation or a washing machine: with an open mind and a grain of salt. Start out with well-known medical institutions, government agencies, and non-profit sites that end in .edu, .gov or .org. Be sure to look for the source of cited information and cross-check it independently. Once you've gotten the lay of the land with your research, start posting questions in forums and make friends who'll help guide the journey (you'll find a vast, helpful community). Link with others on social networking sites to create your own tribe of support, information, and feedback. You'll start to build relationships, a skill level, and a list of go-to sites that will make you more comfortable and savvy over time. (For a specific illness, you may want to start with Curetogether.com, where users offer ratings that compare the "real-world performance of treatments across 600 health conditions." Inspire.com is another online resource, where communities are formed around a specific illness.)

Some great "go-to" places for a newbie to start are the Empowered Patient Coalition (EmpoweredPatientCoalition.org), a basic portal run by Julia Hallisy. Hallisy, a dentist, became a passionate advocate for patients while helping her daughter, Kate, who had been diagnosed at five months of age with a rare cancer of the eyes. Kate died just short of her eleventh birthday. The site offers current links to more than a hundred vetted websites, with both advocate-generated links and trusted medical sources like the Mayo Clinic and the CDC. It also links to nearly two hundred patient advocates from around the country, searchable by state. (See the list in Resources.) Another is AdovateDirectory.org, which casts a broad net to include all kinds of state-by-state resources to patients and families. It's run by Helen Haskell of Mothers Against Medical Error. Also check out CautiousPatient.org, developed by Cari Oliver, an attorney, practicing physician and passionate patient advocate. The site offers many free downloads of strategies and tools for patients. If you're looking to forge grassroots collaborative alliances, you can learn a lot from Patty Skolnik and her organization, Citizens for Patient Safety (citizensforpatientsafety.org).

That's hundreds of links—and only a fraction of what your Internet search might turn up. Imagine if we added links to hospitals, insurers, for-profits, products, and vendors? The unsophisticated user will quickly drown in data.

Putting Patients at the Center of Technologies, Too

The concept of an Internet platform also offers an analogy for how the whole framework of health care might well be redesigned to focus on patients. David "Doc" Searles, a renowned technology guru, pleaded for this re-design in 2008 after his painful encounter with a medical procedure. He was bewildered and disempowered by the fact technologies don't talk to each other:

I believe the closed and proprietary nature of heath care is itself a disease that needs to be cured. That belief came to me during the past week, which I spent in the hospital recovering from an attack of pancreatitis.

[A] probe injected a dye into the [pancreatic] duct, examined the duct from the inside, washed it back out, and retreated. Nothing was found.

There is a 1-in-20 chance that this procedure can cause pancreatitis…Yet for me the chance of getting pancreatitis was 1-in-1. Could we have known that? I believe we could have made a more educated guess than the 1-in-20 template alone provided. The fault there is partly mine, because I knew (and cared) more about myself than the medical system did, and there were possible risk factors which, in retrospect, I should have flagged. But I trusted the system. Thus I found what I should have known first: that the system is built to treat templates, not the pile of combined oddities and typicalities that comprise a sixty-year-old human being.

It also turned out that the procedure was unnecessary. When a second team of doctors looked at the MRI, they said it was clear to them that the cyst wasn't involved with the duct. But that information came too late. I blame myself for that too, because I was in a rush to get the procedure out of the way before a month of long-planned travel. (All of which had to be scuttled, at no small cost.)

Then there was the MRI itself. When we first brought the CD from the MRI facility to our gastroenterologist, it failed to load on her Windows workstation. That was the first delay. Later at home I tried to view the CD but only found a pile of Windows binaries. I only run Linux and Mac machines here. Why weren't the image files in an open format that any machine can view?

The answer came from one of the many doctors that came by my room in the course of my eight days in the hospital. He said that the health care system is collection of closed alliances between large providers of equipment, software systems, and institutional customers. These alliances are closed and proprietary by nature and policy, and account for much of the friction built into the overall health care system—not to mention injuries and deaths due to poor communicating and data sharing among systems and practitioners ...

More than a year ago, Joe Andrieu put the challenge and the solution rather well in a post titled "VRM: The User as Point of Integration." Making the user the point of integration, he said, "has the potential to be profoundly different and profoundly more efficient than current practices."

Applied in the marketplace, it works like this:

Instead of thinking of humans as the active element, think of humans as the environment and vendors as the ants. Instead of humans visiting a bunch of isolated data silos, invert it so that vendors are visiting stationary users—or their stationary data stores...[73]

This philosophy parallels the e-Patients Group (e-Patients.net). Founder Tom Ferguson coined the term "e-Patients" to describe individuals who are *equipped, enabled, empowered and engaged* in their health and health care decisions. He envisioned health care as an equal partnership between e-Patients and health professionals and systems that support them."[74]

We patients should all be thankful that tech-savvy people like Dave deBronkart (e-Patient Dave), the e-Patient movement, and those at the Society for Participatory Medicine (SFPM) are driving the "best practices" bus in the online patient-engagement world. They're a bunch of smart, high-energy people who ferret out and share the latest medical research or new nugget of progress the moment it appears in the cyber world. Many were among the earliest users of internet technology. Through their social media skills, they continue to build a broad and robust community. Because they're dealing with facts they can cite and produce, they're also forging a new level of engagement and respect with physicians (many of whom are also Society members). You and I will benefit from the trail blazing and collaborative culture of these e-pioneers. Think about joining the conversations on their websites

(www.e-patients.net, www.participatorymedicine.org. Full disclosure: I recently signed on as a SFPM member—these folks have a lot to teach!)

But until and unless we have some kind of "one-stop" patient-friendly website for all things medical (as we do for all things "IKEA furniture"), you as a patient or patient advocate need to be your own aggregator and filter. If you're facing a health care challenge and are researching your condition and treatment (and good for you if you are), distill the body of information down to as complete and simple a picture as you can. Then— and only then (physicians will be grateful if you do it this way)—bring any conflicts, questions, or disconnects to your doctor. (Note: Accountable Care Organizations and the Patient Centered Medical Home are redefining the doctor-patient relationship. We look at both in Chapter 6.)

MAKING SENSE OF SO MANY MEDICAL WEBSITES:

Critical Opportunities for Health Care:

1. **Embrace that patients are scouring the Internet.** If they find something new or obscure before you do, welcome the knowledge.
2. **Experiment with social media.** The more people playing with the concept, the sooner we'll find a way to make it cost-effective for you to participate.
3. **Invest a little time in curating your own suggested list of online resources, including patient-support groups for particular diagnoses.** Create a free download to the information on your website. (Don't have one? Consider getting one.)

Critical Opportunities for Patients & Families

1. **You can find almost anything on the Internet. Not all of it's true or helpful.** Crosscheck what you find with other sources.
2. **Don't panic when online message boards paint a grim picture of your diagnosis.** People who have successful outcomes often get busy doing other things and stop posting.
3. **Investigate choices that don't involve surgery or drugs.** They're usually not supported by medical literature because there's no

money in funding studies. Curetogether.com may offer insights, and Inspire.com will take you to a community of people with the same condition. A good physician will be willing to discuss what you find.

4. **Don't show up at the doctor's office with the kind of printouts and ratings you'd bring to the new car dealer, or ask for that new drug or treatment you've convinced yourself you need.** Make sense of your research by distilling key questions and concerns to raise with your care provider, before drawing conclusions about your treatment options.

4 If IKEA designed health care...

we'd get tools for success when we walked in the door

Why does IKEA invest in providing customers with bags, catalogs, measuring tapes, pencils, lists, maps, and carts—before they even walk onto the showroom floor? Because they want them to have tools for success: to accomplish their goals and to have satisfying, stress-free experiences (which in turn facilitates satisfaction and sales).

IKEA designs its tables, bookcases, and even sofas so you can put the whole thing together with a simple Allen wrench. Then they make sure you have the Allen wrench: it's sealed in the carton. And there's a supply of twine at the loading dock to secure items to the roof of your car. (Imagine millions of IKEA customers every day fumbling around for paper and pencil, store map, Allen wrench, and twine?) IKEA has clearly thought through not just how to design and deploy products you'll want, but how to make tools available where and when you need them. They are your partner in maximizing your success not just while in the building, but *once you've left the store.*

In contrast, think of the hospital patient. As a marketing executive at a major hospital group described to me a couple of years ago, "there are two groups of people in this country who enter big institutions and are forced to hand over to strangers all their personal things, stripped of everything that gives them identity and comfort: their clothes, wallet, jewelry, shoes, and underwear—even their eyeglasses and dentures. One group is prisoners. The other is hospital patients."

I recognized this stunningly simple truth from the months my father had been hospitalized. If there's a more disempowering experience a person can go through, I can't imagine it. We are totally at the whim of others for health, food, water, bathroom, information, and attention. How easily we can become convinced we don't matter that much.

And this is just the introductory phase of our stay. Once we're "in the system," the environments we live in can be even more disempowering.

Designing for Dignity

"Smart people can sometimes be remarkably stupid," says designer Michael Graves.

You may know Graves as the guy who brought sleek, affordable design to everyday items we can buy at Target (like a tea kettle or a telephone). In 2003, a rare illness left him paralyzed from the chest down. He was thrust into life in a wheelchair—and into a world of bad design. (He often tells the story of lying on a hospital gurney after a night of excruciating pain, thinking only, "I don't want to die here…because it's so ugly.") Spending three years in eight hospitals and three rehab centers, trying to adjust to life in a wheelchair, inspired Graves to design better tools for patients. "They didn't make big mistakes…they just made the most frustrating mistakes you could ever imagine, and made your cure more difficult. Your room should make it easier for the doctors and the aides and the patient. But instead it does just the opposite."[75]

At a rehabilitation center, for instance, Graves wheeled himself into the bathroom one morning. When he reached for the sink faucet for hot water, the handle was out of reach. So was the toothbrush and toothpaste. He looked for an outlet for his electric razor. The outlet was near the base of the wall near the floor—also out of his reach from the wheelchair. The biggest aggravation, he said, was that the rehabilitation center was *built* for people in wheelchairs. "When I went through some of the struggles that were caused by my room, I lost the self-empowerment that I was supposedly gaining during the days in rehabilitation," said Graves. "I was no longer self-reliant, but dependent. This makes you feel terrible as a patient—as a paraplegic. You're feeling at the will of others." He stayed at one glossy, new hospital with a four-story glass atrium and expansive lobbies. But that hospital's patient rooms were so small that those in wheelchairs and hospital employees had a hard time maneuvering.[76]

"All the money had been spent on the public spaces," he said. "The public spaces were glorious. I got to the patient room—these were the smallest patient rooms ever known to man." Channeling all his frustration, Graves continued to sketch better ways to design the hospital—furniture, rooms, buildings. The bed table he ultimately designed takes into account the need for patients to have two surfaces: one for when the meal tray is brought in, and the other for personal items. The cart he designed has a drawer that opens on both sides, a lidded plastic drawer that the patient can take home with them, and an attached litterbin. He added a simple but effective pair of catches on the back of a hospital chair, so that a sheet on the chair actually stays put, rather than falling on the floor.

Thanks to a deal with the hospital-furnishing company Stryker, some of these products became available in 2009.

With his democratic, attractive, human-centered design, Graves has come up with the kind of furniture IKEA might strive to create if it turned its attention to hospitals. On a more basic level, he and others designing from the patient's point of view understand the power of good design: it can actually make the right behaviors a little easier, and the wrong ones harder. What works better for the patient tends to work for the provider, and vice versa.

An entire industry has grown up around finding these solutions. It's called human factors engineering: designing tools and environments to work in tandem with what we do naturally.

Mousetraps and Swiss Cheese

Remember playing the game of Mousetrap when you were a kid? You'd set up a contraption of interconnecting plastic pieces on the game board, and perch a marble on top. Turn a crank, and the marble rolls down a plank, into a bathtub, drops through a hole, and winds its way through a series of adventures that ultimately lowers a cage on the mouse. The system is designed to work the same way every time, relying on simple physics. In its own elegant way, the design of the "Mousetrap" environment represents a systematic approach to achieving predictable outcomes.

In health care or any complex system, the goal is for the "marble"—the task or procedure—to get to the desired outcome as consistently and effortlessly as possible. Any glitches or bumps along the path are identified and eliminated, to make the path to success as frictionless as possible. When it works, the IV is always inserted properly because all components are available, the doctor accesses critical patient data with a few intuitive clicks, and patients find their way to the radiology department without asking three times for directions.

But when designing systems to *prevent* an event, like an infection or a wrong-site surgery, the challenge is to erect multiple *barriers,* any one of which can stop that marble from rolling on through.

The "Swiss cheese model", widely embraced as a mental model for preventing organizational accidents, is the opposite of the Mousetrap model. I first heard about the "Swiss cheese" model in a speech by Robert Wachter MD, a national expert on patient safety. The idea is that a single error is rarely enough to cause harm. Instead, such errors have to penetrate multiple incomplete layers of protection (layers of Swiss cheese) to cause a devastating result. The thinking goes that rather than focusing on the (futile) goal of trying to make humans behave perfectly, we try to "shrink the holes in the cheese" by creating multiple overlapping layers of protection.[77]

The medical world tries to analyze and correct the "root causes" that allowed the error to "get through" the layers of Swiss cheese. Were surgical checklists used? Was housekeeping too busy to adequately clean the surfaces in the patient's room, allowing the transfer of infectious bacteria? Was the resident too tired to think clearly? Did the person inserting the IV line clean their hands properly? Was the young nurse too intimidated to speak up when she suspected an error? Any one of these people might have stopped the harm from happening; the failure of each to do so allows the harm to "get through."

The Mousetrap and the Swiss cheese scenarios are places where patients and their advocates, given the right tools, can help. In the Mousetrap model, they might be given a printout of their own medical record (or access to it online) to review for inaccuracies, a process called "open notes".[78] In the Swiss cheese model, they can help plug the holes in the cheese. This might mean giving patients hand sanitizing wipes as a guard against infection, and encouraging them to use them.

IKEA has designed its own "Mousetrap" scenario. Its offering of "everything under one roof"—from beds, to bedding, to the utensils for breakfast in bed, to the breakfast, to the maps that guide you along the route, to on-site child care and even the twine provided in the loading bays—is designed to be a "frictionless" approach to getting predictable and desired outcomes. The tools and amenities ensure customers will stay longer, buy more, and leave happier. In medical care, we saw an example of this in chapter 1 with Laura Esserman's "everything under one roof" breast cancer clinic. It meant designing an environment that anticipated and addressed the patient's medical needs, emotions and stress level. The approach "smoothed the path" to the desired outcome: giving the patient good, expedient care, dignity, respect and control.

This kind of work, providing patients with the tools needed for success, takes vision, leadership and resources. Unfortunately, hospitals are unlikely to run out and replace their current inventory of furniture with Michael Graves-designed pieces. And achieving Esserman's patient-centered vision was years in the making and required putting up a new building.

So what *can* hospitals provide to equip patients with essential tools for success (and what should patients equip themselves with if they're not made available)?

Feel free to skip ahead to the suggestions at the end of this chapter, but real insight comes by walking in the patient's shoes.

First, walk the halls of the hospital, imagining you don't know where things are and don't know the staff. Is the signage clear? Is the staff wearing badges, so you can tell a doctor from a transport worker?

Now you're an admitted patient. For every test, every procedure, transport services will come and fetch you and "hand you off" to a new team. Your chart may be the only constant, the only thing sure to stay with you (unless it's an electronic record, with may yield new efficiencies but will likely come with new problems, which makes the case for some kind of tangible personal health record). What about your personal stuff? When your procedure is completed, will you be returned to the same room? If not, who packs up your things? Who makes sure your dentures and eyeglasses don't get lost? (During my mother's recent hospitalization her room was changed six times in five days). Should a checklist of critical patient items accompany the chart?

Now imagine you're a patient in a bed, alone, in pain, staring at the ceiling tiles. You have lots of questions. You're afraid you'll forget them or you'll be asleep when the doctor comes in. Is there a way to put up a note? Lots of people have been touching you, and touching your stuff, and shaking your hand, and you have no way to clean your own hands. Your cell phone rings, but it's across the room...somebody moved the bed table out of reach. You hesitate to hit the call button...the nurses are so busy...

What is your treatment plan for today, or for the duration? Is there a white board in your room? Did the nurses write anything on it? Can you reach it, so you can write notes on it yourself?

Then there are procedures that can be painful, difficult or even dangerous if you're not coached on what will happen and how to cooperate. Recently my friend Noel had extensive surgery in a top east coast hospital. At one point he needed a nasogastric tube, a long thin tube inserted through the nose and down into the stomach to carry food and medicine. The insertion is made easier when the patient drinks water the whole time, because the process of swallowing helps ease the tube into place. However the nurse in charge told Noel only to "take a sip of water" as the tube was inserted. Not being told the reason behind it, the insertion was painful, led to a severe nosebleed, and added strain to Noel's already frail health. "I should have been given something to read about the procedure," he says, "or even better, shown a video so I'd understand how to cooperate." Similarly, when my brother had a procedure to see if cancer had invaded his pancreas, it led to a bout of pancreatitis (inflammation of the pancreas), which is a very common side effect and extremely painful. He writhed in agony for hours that night because the staff could not reach the physician to order a pain medication. If my brother and his family had been advised prior to the procedure this was a likely outcome, perhaps handed an advisory or shown a video, would the issue of pain control have been more likely to come up and be addressed?

Finally, it's discharge day. Yay! You're handed a sheet of instructions, prescription orders to fill, notes about following up, and several brochures. You nod your head in agreement and stuff it all in the plastic drawstring bag along with your pink water pitcher and dirty laundry. What are the odds you'll remember what you're told?

All these scenarios are fraught with challenge—and opportunity. Some hospitals have come up with good solutions.[79] They may report on their successes in journals, blogs, and at conferences. But in the wild wild west of health care, there's no central "best practices" repository where you can find them (though the Institute for Healthcare Improvement may come closest), and no organization responsible or accountable for system-wide adoption. Simply asking patients how well things are working may offer the best solutions.

If IKEA was in the health care business, you can imagine how it might design intuitive, affordable and integrated "fixes" for these challenges. They would "smooth the path" for patients so they could help themselves achieve desired outcomes. In this way they'd be engineering for predictable, systematic success.

Designing with respect for patients' capacity to participate, and to empower us with independence and autonomy, is the best—and kindest— way to engage us as active partners in our care.

GIVING PATIENTS TOOLS FOR SUCCESS WHEN THEY WALK IN THE DOOR:

Critical Opportunities for Health Care

1. **Provide a way to clean hands.**
2. **Give basic tips to patients,** such as the warning signs of infection the patient should look out for. Redness, swelling, or heat at an

IV site is something a nurse might miss. A patient or advocate can offer another set of eyes and ears.

3. **Provide a "dashboard" for patients, with critical information posted in every patient room plus the hospital emergency room.** This might include the name of the nurse and physician attending you, the person in charge, and how to reach them.

4. **Provide a notepad and pen.** In hotel rooms there's a complimentary pad of paper and a pen. But when you go in the hospital, where the cost of a night's stay runs into the thousands of dollars, there's no paper or pen in sight. When the nurse discusses instructions about your care, or the doctor arrives to tell you the results of your MRI, it's not a time for you or your advocate to be scrambling for a scrap of paper and a pen.

5. **Provide a place to keep personal items accessible and safe.** Hospitals lose tens of thousands of dollars' worth of patients' items each year. In addition their lost-and-founds are well stocked with hearing aids, dentures, eyeglasses, and other items precious to the patient, and to no one else. Many of these items, often unwittingly left on dinner trays or on top of beds, are either tossed out in the kitchen trash or bundled up with soiled linens.[80] In my father's case, his hearing aids became water-damaged shortly after he was admitted to the hospital. He spent most of his hospitalization unable to hear what people were saying to him.[81] These items also get lost in the shuffle when a patient is moved from room to room. This speaks to the need for a system (perhaps a checklist, or designated person on each floor) who ensures all personal items are kept together and that they move with the patient.

6. **Designate a default "communication space" (such as a whiteboard) within reach of the patient to make their goals, questions and concerns visible to any member of the care team who enters the room.**

7. **Consider a physical system to manage discharge materials.** On "discharge day," we patients are handed a bunch of paperwork, including follow-up instructions, copies of forms, prescriptions, and pamphlets. We hope it all makes it home and that when we

get there, we'll remember and understand everything we were told. That's a lot to leave to chance. Consider a binder, folder, or packet that keeps these important papers contained and accessible.

8. **Inform us patients of how we can make a procedure more tolerable or successful.** When problems are predictable consider a scripted advisory, spoken or printed, or a video.

Critical Opportunities for Patients & Families

1. **Don't assume that the items described above will be provided.** Ask first. If they're not, bring them yourself and use them often.

2. **Give feedback on how well your environment, furnishings and the tools provided worked (or didn't work) for you.** Share with the staff how and why something extra provided to you, such as a packet of hand wipes, or a notepad and pen, made a difference. The hospital's Value Analysis Committee analyzes and approves or rejects all expenditures, based on their relative and proven value. Let your voice be among the influencers.

3. **Bring a bit of the familiar with you**. "After a while, you stop feeling human", says my friend Noel. Listen to favorite music or stream your favorite radio program (if the hospital has WiFi) on your Mp3 (be careful not to leave any valuables out when you're not there). If you'll be in the hospital for awhile, bring loose pajama bottoms, a bathrobe, your pillow (with a different-colored pillowcase so you can spot it upon discharge) and sturdy, comfy slippers. (Noel loved his faux-fur-lined Crocs). Don't forget the charger for your phone and other electronic devices, an extension cord if needed, and earphones or earbuds. Personal photos displayed around the room can perk you up and humanize you to others. Bring your own toiletries, like deodorant, lip balm, soap, and toothpaste. Watch videos, listen to podcasts or read books that make you laugh—laughter is one of the best medicines of all.

5

If IKEA designed health care...

we customers
would have to
roll up our
sleeves and help

In order to give many people a better everyday life, IKEA asks the customer to work as a partner. For example, by assembling the furniture yourself, we are able to offer it at a low price.

—from the IKEA website

The concept of customer as partner in forging the value proposition may not be unique to IKEA. However, as a mainstream business familiar to consumers, as well as to many organizations that provide goods and services to them, the IKEA model offers important insights.

IKEA stumbled upon a key driver of value proposition by accident and ran with it. Its "flat pack" innovation was borne of a frustration experienced by an early employee of the company. After struggling to squeeze a table into the trunk of his car, he decided to take its legs off. Separated into five pieces, the table fit—and flat-pack furniture was invented. Today, the ideas of "flat-pack" and "IKEA" are inseparable. This saves transportation, storage, assembly, and delivery costs—which are passed on to the consumer.

In exchange, you, the customer, are given a lot of work to do. You have to drive to the store, find what you want, gather the pieces and boxes in the warehouse, lug the stuff to the cash register, load it on top of the car, tie it down, haul it home, and put it together.[82]

Of course affordability is a big reason IKEA products are so popular. Whether it's the relentless drive to keep the cost of products down, founder Kamprad's "Horatio Alger" story that fueled IKEA's rise to power, or some combination, the frugality at the company's core also seems to resonate.[83]

Thrift is the core of IKEA's corporate culture. Michael Ohlsson (Chief Executive Officer) of IKEA Group traces it back to the company's origins in Smaland, a poor region in southern Sweden whose inhabitants, he says, are "stubborn, cost-conscious, and ingenious at making a living with very little." Ever since Ingvar Kamprad founded IKEA in 1943, the company has tried to allow "people with limited means to furnish their houses like rich people."

"We hate waste," says Ohlsson. He points proudly at a bright-red "Ektorp" sofa. Last year his designers found a way to pack the popular three-seater more compactly, doubling the amount of sofa they could cram into a given space. That shaved €100 ($135) from the price tag—and significantly reduced the carbon-dioxide emissions from transporting it...

—"The Secret of IKEA's Success," The Economist, February 24, 2011

In health care, a patient or "customer" has much more at stake than buying furniture and thus much more to lose. Yet our health care system has barely required—or even asked for—patients to participate in the "value proposition."

That's beginning to change—not just because insurance is covering less and less of our medical expenses, or because empowered patients themselves are asking questions and insisting on shared decision-making with like-minded physicians.[84] It's also because, as with IKEA and elsewhere, the promise of money in their pocket can get people to change their behavior.

Most of the financial incentive so far is offered via employers. And they're finding it's a good investment. Employees enrolled in workplace wellness programs report reduced personal health care costs, most commonly because of fitness-center discounts and free preventative screenings. For instance, according to the findings of a January 2012 survey by Principal Financial Group reported in *USA Today*, employers who invest in wellness programs see increased employee retention, attendance, and productivity. The numbers show that medical costs improve "by an average of $3.27, and absenteeism costs improve by an average of $2.73 for every dollar spent on wellness." As one reporter observed: "The real motivator for Americans to get fit at work isn't smaller jeans—it's a bigger bank balance."[85]

So far, large corporations have led the charge. But according to the survey, small and midsize businesses are trying to catch up; just ask their employees. Of the 1,121 wellness-program participants surveyed, over half said they are more productive as a result, 40 percent agreed that wellness programs encourage them to stay with their company, and more than a third said they have missed fewer days of work.

We Love The Things We Make

"Look what I made!" we say with pride, whether it's a five-year-old pointing to her Lego creation or a grownup presenting a perfect soufflé. When it comes to investing in creating something, we love the things we make. Researchers at Yale University and Duke University tested this theory with college students. The students were asked to assemble IKEA boxes, fold origami, build sets of Legos, and then to bid on their own creations, along with other people's, to demonstrate conditions for "the IKEA effect—the increase in valuation of self-made products". The results: "participants saw their amateurish creations as similar in value to experts' creations, and expected others to share their opinions."[86]

Is there a similar satisfaction in co-creating our own good health outcome? We all know someone who dug into the hard work of fixing their diet and taking up exercise to beat back health problems, and succeeded. They feel great about it, and justifiably so. If we want a holistic and efficient partnership in health care, it requires patients doing our part, too. Did we take the initiative to eat right and do our physical therapy prior to our surgery? Did we follow the doctor's advice and quit smoking after our cancer surgery? Do we bear some responsibility for our diabetes, or need for a knee replacement, as a consequence of our morbid obesity? Whether it's cigarettes, fatty foods, excessive alcohol, or limiting our exercise to channel surfing, we are responsible for tempting the odds of having chronic health diseases like diabetes and heart disease.[87] "I sometimes feel like patients are telling me they want me to make them stop bleeding, but without pulling out the arrows stuck in their chests," says Dr. Lee Green, professor of family medicine at the University of Michigan in Ann Arbor.[88]

It's a free country, and we patients don't need or want the "health police" telling us what we can or can't do. For many patients, cultural and educational factors also create an added challenge. But it's hard to blame those making more responsible choices if they're resentful of paying for the care of those who make poor ones (which is how insurance works).

If IKEA designed health care, we'd all lie down in the bed we made.

The "IKEA" of Hospitals

U.S. health care might see a further example of "partnership with patients" in the approach of an inspiring, charismatic doctor, half a world away.

In India, private financing—out-of-pocket dollars—makes up 78 percent of total health spending, among the highest percentages in the world. Approximately 40 percent of India's population has to either borrow money or sell possessions to pay for hospitalization. Each year, nearly a quarter of the population falls into poverty due to medical expenses.[88]

Indian cardiac surgeon Dr. Devi Shetty may have found a solution, at least for the two million Indians each year that need heart surgery. Shetty, who came to world attention in the 1990s as cardiologist to Mother Theresa, is chairman and founder of the Narayana Hrudayalaya Hospitals in Bengaluru. At the group's flagship 1,000-bed "heart factory," open-heart surgery costs $2,000, on average, for procedures that US hospitals are paid between $20,000 and $50,000, depending on the complexity of the surgery.[89]

Dr. Shetty continues to drive cost savings (and affordable access to care) at new hospitals he's building across India. He is currently building a new 300-bed heart hospital in Mysore. Such a hospital would cost nearly 1.37 billion INR, or Indian Rupees ($30 million), and take three years to build. By contrast Shetty announced that his facility will take a maximum of five months at a cost of 183 million INR ($4 million). This new hospital will allow him to offer open-heart surgery at a cost of 36,660 INR ($800). Quite a feat, considering the cheapest of these procedures cost ten times that amount in the US. How is Shetty accomplishing this?

By teaming up with the largest construction company in India. The new building will be a ground floor facility; multiple-story buildings cost more to build. According to Shetty, the new design allows for good ventilation and sunlight, thereby cutting back on power requirements. After initial training, family members are responsible for non-technical care—making the bed, fetching water, and emptying a bedpan.

> *Shetty was surgeon to Mother Teresa, who, he says, taught him that to achieve something big, it need not be complicated. Indeed, his simple model may have the potential to revolutionize the way health care is delivered in low-income settings. Narayana Hrudayalaya exudes an aura of simplicity, despite the abundance of state-of-the-art technology and techniques employed there. It is better organized and notably calmer than other hospitals.*[90]
>
> —"Revolutionizing Health Care for the Poor,"
> *The Guardian,* January 21, 2011

What Makes a Good Advocate?

In the United States, hands-on family/advocate participation in hospital patient care runs the gamut. Many newer hospital designs (especially children's and maternity hospitals) include a foldout bed for an overnight guest and promote a culture where family engagement is encouraged (see chapter 1). Some patients do not have anyone willing or able to act as their advocates, which accounts for a growing body of professional patient advocates (see link to national database at www.advoconnect.com). And some facilities strictly limit family visiting hours and overnight stays, even when a patient wants their advocate to stay (though in recent months more hospitals have begun relaxing their visitor policies.)

Furthermore, advocates are not created equal. Martin J. Hatlie, CEO of Project Patient Care, a Chicago-based advocacy group and a nationally recognized leader in patient advocacy, says "being a good patient advocate takes a combination of skills—teamwork skills. By all means be a partner—but don't be afraid to be a 'pushy' one."

"There are certain things as a layperson that you won't immediately understand," Hatlie says, "such as why the patient is suddenly spiking a fever. Be respectful," he says, "in asking a physician or nurse to explain. But remember—physicians and nurses may have more expertise, but they are not decision-makers. The patient is, and if you are the patient's caregiver, you are the patient's agent. Bottom line, this is our healthcare system, and providers work for us."

Members of the medical team are taught to be assertive, says Hatlie, especially when there is a safety concern. Advocates should think of themselves as on par with the medical team in this respect. 'I do understand the hospital has a rule against staying overnight in a patient's room,' you might say, 'but might an exception be made? My friend is really anxious.' That's an advocate you want at your side—someone who plays well with others but has a backbone."

Sometimes it helps to have more than one advocate. If you're a direct person, Hatlie says, recruit someone with a softer approach. When he was a caregiver for a very sick parent, Hatlie fired her doctor immediately after their first meeting. This was in a hospital setting. "I knew she wasn't the right doctor for my Mom, and was honest about that. But I knew the doctor might be embarrassed and we might be labeled a 'difficult' family. So, my siblings and their spouses got in action and went out of their way to show appreciation. They thanked people. They noticed details and called them to the staff's attention—like a nearly empty IV bag or nearly full urine container. They helped Mom to the bathroom and did other small things so the staff would be free for other tasks. They'd compliment caregivers who performed their jobs conscientiously, like the nurse who finds a vein with little discomfort on the first try. We saw things every day that could have been done better," say Hatlie, "but we were kind to the people who were kind to us. We made ourselves a part of their team—all on the same side, the patient's side."

But when it comes to *whether* you should have an advocate with you in the first place? "One thing that I tell people is, if you have a sick family member, don't leave them alone in the hospital," says physician Atul Gawande. "Even when there are visiting hours where you're supposed to go home, I'll tell people, find any way you can to stay anyway, because when you're sick is the last moment when, as a patient, you're able to fend for yourself. And the family member is often the person, as shifts change and different people come and go, who will be the one to convey, 'You know, my dad actually seems sicker than he did yesterday.' You'll be surprised about the extent to which just having those kinds of eyes and ears are missing with the slew of people coming and going. So I know it can be unnerving. It's sort of like when the effort to trap terrorists falls through, and the passenger has to be the one to tackle the terrorist trying to light the bomb on the plane."[92]

In light of our earlier look at hospital hierarchies, and the intimidation they breed, is expecting a patient or advocate to speak up or "be pushy" a bit unrealistic? A May 2012 Health Affairs report hints our deference to providers runs deep. In focus groups with 48 people, it found even "relatively affluent and well-educated patients feel compelled to conform to socially sanctioned roles and defer to physicians during clinical consultations; that physicians can be authoritarian; and that the fear of being categorized as 'difficult' prevents patients from participating more fully in their own health care." [93] (More on this in chapter 7.)

Hatlie says that's exactly *why* we need someone on our side. "Patients themselves are different," he says. "They do worry about getting labeled as difficult and getting poorer quality care as a result. No question. And I don' t think we can ask patients to take on the work of changing culture. It's just too much when they are sick or injured. But I feel advocates are in a different position. They can push the envelope. I still think they should be very respectful in doing so – 'golden rule', that's how they'd want to be treated if the were the healthcare workers. But that said, family members need to be direct when there is a safety issue. That's what we're teaching in teamwork training…It may feel like one is being disruptive, but you'll be earning respect…so, I think we should be pushy. In the nicest possible way, of course."[94]

Outsourcing the Helper's Role

What if you don't know anyone who would make a good advocate for you, don't want to ask, or need a little extra help? More and more folks are turning to professional patient advocates. Many have medical and/or business training and can help with a range of needs, from advocating directly at the bedside and quarterbacking the care team to resolving billing issues. They're entirely focused on your needs—not the hospital's, doctor's or insurance company's—and can provide welcome clarity and focus during times of high emotion and stress.

The cost varies according to the service, but for now it's all out-of-pocket. *Your* pocket. Why should you pay for it? Says Trisha Torrey, who runs AdvoConnection (AdvoConnection.com) a national directory of patient advocates, "for the same reason you'd use a real estate broker to buy a home, or a CPA to do your taxes. You could do it yourself...but what if something went wrong? You don't know what you don't know - but professionals do know because they deal in it every day."

Families as True Partners

Sadly, too many of us family members don't appreciate the proactive role we might have played, until a poor outcome makes us wish we'd understood what was at stake. Then our "participatory" role can take on an entirely new and tragic dimension. Patty Skolnik of Denver, whom we met in the introduction of this book, spent months caring for her son Michael after unnecessary brain surgery rendered him a paraplegic. During various stages, until his death, she would clean his tracheotomy site, suction his mouth, diaper and comfort him, often relying on nurses only when a more sophisticated nursing task was needed. "In all those years," Patty says, "we only had one bad doctor—the one who told Michael he needed the surgery and got him to sign the consent form, while our son was on meds, and after we'd gone home for the night. All our son's other caregivers were wonderful." As mentioned earlier in this book, Patty now speaks on patient/provider collaboration around the world.

Helen Haskell, Mary Ellen Mannix, and John James also would have done anything—hands-on or otherwise—to save their children.

But they were not embraced as collaborative partners on their children's respective care team. Helen, whom you met in the introduction, is a nationally recognized patient advocate and founder of Mothers Against Medical Error (MAME). She lost her 15-year-old son Lewis to blood loss and infection following elective, corrective surgery on his chest. A pain medication he was given ate a hole in his stomach. He died of blood loss and infection over the next 30 hours, while Helen couldn't get the care team to take her growing concerns seriously. Mary Ellen's baby, James, was diagnosed before he was born with a heart defect that's normally uncomplicated to repair. As Mary Ellen relates, "despite this advance knowledge, James' cardiac team never told us, his parents, they would be performing the most aggressive surgery possible on our newborn. James was then put on a known broken ventilator, quickly taken off it, then left unattended during the crucial hours after his open-heart surgery. James died at eleven days old due to these multiple medical errors brought on by poor communication."[95] John James lost his nineteen-year-old son, John Alexander James, as a result of "uninformed, careless, and unethical care by cardiologists," according to his father. His son had collapsed while running and self-recovered, but was subsequently taken by ambulance to his college town hospital. He was sent home five days later with a clean bill of health. Less than three weeks later he collapsed and died while running.[96]

If Patty, Helen, Mary Ellen, and John had been embraced as participants on the care team—consulted and respected in real time about their concerns and knowledge of their children—might they have had different outcomes? Though that painful question can never be answered, they've worked tirelessly trying to win all of us that right for *our* children. Encouragingly, their work is making a difference *inside* medical circles.

Helen, Mary Ellen and John recently collaborated with Dr. David Mayer, then at the Institute for Patient Safety Excellence in Chicago, on a landmark article about family involvement in medical care. The article, written in the journal *Progress in Pediatric Cardiology* and published in February 2012 by Elsevier (publishers of the Lancet), is entitled "Parents and Families as Partners in the Care of Pediatric Cardiology Patients."[97]

Though the document (excerpted below) addresses parents and children, it serves as a blueprint for the inclusion of any patient advocate or family member.

1. **Ensure that parents have the information they need.** "Familiarize advocates with the dangers of hospital-acquired infection and equip parents and families with tools such as bleach wipes (which kill spore-forming *C. diff*) to sanitize the environment..."

2. **Respect the knowledge that parents and families possess.** "... To overlook the detailed personal knowledge of a parent of a child with a serious medical condition is to disregard a rich source of information that has a direct bearing upon the course of that child's treatment...Older children know their own bodies best, parents know their children's behavioral norms, and physicians bring the technical knowledge to heal. By working together, the healing of a young heart has a better chance of happening."

3. **Respect parents' need to know the cost of testing and procedures.** "...Under the current medical system in the United States, the fear of ruinous medical bills pervades the middle class and is the second leading cause of fear behind loss of retirement funds for those with health insurance...Parents need to be cognizant of the costs of procedures and informed until they understand that the cost-effectiveness of proposed diagnostic or interventional procedures is justified."

4. **Educate parents on potential complications to watch for.** "... Shared decision making is a process, not an event, and should continually reset expectations as the care of the child evolves...For most parents, it is helpful to have a written list. At home, parents need a number to call for questions and a 24-hour number for urgent concerns; in the hospital, they need to be briefed on the procedure for dealing with emergencies (e.g., a rapid response team) and how they as parents should go about accessing these mechanisms if their bedside nurse is not available."

5. **Smooth the path of communication.** "...Minimize barriers to direct communication. This includes being sure the parent is

explicitly provided with an e-mail address for the child's doctor and with a telephone number that the parent understands can be called at all hours, even from the hospital...Finally, it should be made clear to nurses and residents that families' questions are to be welcomed. The model of trying to 'protect the attending physician from being called at home' is not patient-centered."

6. **Create a family-centered culture.** "...Seek patient and family input into programs and policies throughout the organization... While caution should obviously be exercised to avoid overburdening families who may already be stretched thin, many family members find it gratifying to share their hard-won wisdom for the benefit of other families...Perhaps most important, patient and family members serve an invaluable role as faculty in classes for students in medicine, nursing, and allied health professions."[98]

The fact that patient advocates' input has been published in an industry journal of the caliber of *Progress in Pediatric Cardiology* is a testament to their years of focused determination and offers hope for the meaningful inclusion of the patient and family voice in health care.

As with IKEA, we have available plenty of tools and information to empower patients as partners and create a "shared value proposition." The more we patients and providers understand each others' respective roles and realities, the better we'll be able to partner with each other effectively.

ASKING PATIENTS TO "ROLL UP THEIR SLEEVES AND HELP":

Critical Opportunities for Health Care

1. **Redefine the customer: "patient" becomes "participant."**
2. **Create a "shared-value proposition"** so that patients and caregivers understand their respective roles and realities.
3. **Respect the information that parents and families possess. Provide** patients with an email address for their doctor and a phone number they can call during an emergency at any hour, even from the hospital.

4. **Provide patients with an email address for their doctor** and a phone number.
5. **Educate patients on potential complications to watch for.**

Critical Opportunities for Patients & Families

1. **Take ownership of your body, choices and outcomes. Be a partner.**
2. **Speak up if someone forgets to wash their hands before touching you, or if some aspect of your care doesn't seem right.** As in any conversation, tone and respect are key.
3. **Read up on hospital-acquired infections and medical harm.** Once you understand how they occur, you'll understand the role you can play in preventing them.
5. **Write down things to alert staff to and post so they'll see it when they arrive.**
6. **Find an advocate who will be pleasant but firm when needed.**
7. **Delegate non-medical tasks to your family member or advocate,** like tidying the bed or getting water. Your busy nursing staff will appreciate it, and you.
8. **Consider setting up an account on CaringBridge.org.** This allows you to keep an on-line journal and guestbook that can be shared with family and friends. Updating the journal regularly saves you from making multiple calls during a stressful time, keeps a record of events, and offers a wider circle of friends and family an opportunity to pass along encouragement and bring up concerns you might have missed.
9. **Consider hiring a professional patient advocate.** Find national data bases of advocates searchable for your area at Advoconnection. com (you'll find a substantial number of Registered Nurse [RN] Patient Advocates) and the Professional Patient Advocate Institute (patientadvocatetraining.com). Kinergy Health (KinergyHealth. com) offers virtual "patient navigators" who will provide skilled assistance with coordinating medical information across the care team, finding resources and identifying services for clients.

6 If IKEA designed health care...

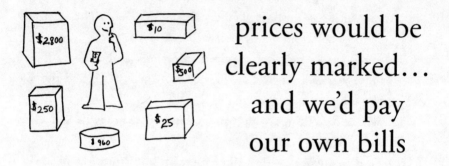

prices would be
clearly marked...
and we'd pay
our own bills

Every item in IKEA stores has a big, black-and-white price tag on it. The tag also displays all product dimensions, the colors it comes in, the alternate dimensions available, and where to find it in the store. You can compare the sofas, the desks, and the kitchen faucets for price versus benefit. This *defines* "transparency."

Health care doesn't even come close. Prices of drugs, treatments, services, and procedures are practically a state secret. Our third-party payment system has historically shielded patients from the true cost of care. Consider some examples, ripped from news headlines:

Obesity surgery for teenagers. *The New York Times* reported on a seventeen-year-old—five feet tall and nearly 300 pounds—who could have lost her excess weight through diet and exercise but didn't try very hard. So a New York State program for low-income people paid $21,369 for an operation whereby a surgeon tightened a silicon band around her stomach to curb feelings of hunger. After losing only thirty-four pounds, the girl began again downing chips and chocolate with abandon—and was almost back to where she started.

Stents for patients with stable heart pain. Patients showing symptoms of a heart attack often undergo angioplasty, involving the insertion of a metal tube called a stent. But about one in eight angioplasties is done on patients with stable angina who show only minor chest pain.[99] One doctor in Maryland reportedly extracted $3.8 million from Medicare for implanting nearly 600 medically unnecessary stents.

MRIs for athletes with minor pains. As an experiment, a Florida sports-medicine orthopedist did MRI scans on thirty-one fit and happy professional baseball pitchers. He found abnormal shoulder cartilage in 90 percent of the athletes. Based on the scans, he could have operated on nine out of ten of them—totally unnecessarily. Insurers pay over $1,000 for an MRI scan.[100]

Over treatment—tests and procedures not only medically unnecessary, but often dangerous—remains a big reason that spending on health care, by families and by the government, is crowding out spending on almost everything else. As a nation, we now spend eighteen percent of our gross domestic product on health care. And incentives to providers pervert these costs.

"We have very perverse incentives," agrees cardiologist and surgeon Steven Nissen, MD, of the Cleveland Clinic. "The way our payment system works is if you put more stents on coronary arteries, you make more money. If you do more studies, you make more money. The physicians are largely well intentioned, but the incentives are driving over-utilization. You're twice as likely to get a CAT scan in the US as you are in most Western European countries. You're twice as likely to have a heart catheterization. Our population isn't that much different." [100]

Rosemary Gibson, who led national quality and safety initiatives at the Robert Wood Johnson Foundation, shared in an email a particularly disturbing example of over-treatment that borders on the criminal:[101]

A few months ago I was introduced to a gentleman who had been a corporate VP for employee benefits at a Fortune 100 company for many years. I was impressed with his knowledge of health care. He shared some of his experiences with company employees, who lived all over the country. The company had a policy that when employees were informed they had a very serious medical condition, the company paid for a second opinion. For example, when employees were told they needed a heart transplant, the company paid the cost for travel and a second opinion at the Mayo Clinic. Mayo found that 40 percent of the transplants that had been recommended to employees were not medically necessary or appropriate.

The VP saw cases in which transplants were recommended for people who were going to die soon from cancer whether the transplant was done or not.

Sometimes hospitals and surgeons were extremely aggressive in promoting transplants that could not possibly be beneficial to the patients. One hospital recommended a heart-lung transplant for a patient. When the patient visited Mayo for a second opinion, it was discovered that neither a heart nor a lung transplant was indicated for the patient. She left the hospital with no surgery.

Another employee was told he needed a heart transplant. When the VP called the surgeon at a well-known institution to tell him that his company will pay for a Mayo second opinion, the surgeon said the patient shouldn't fly on a plane in his condition. In fact, the employee had just traveled on a plane to see the surgeon and was happy to go to Mayo for a second opinion. The second opinion revealed a small blockage that was successfully managed with a stent.

The VP said the team in his company that worked with Mayo had a wall of cards and notes from grateful employees. The employees who were spared massive surgeries called the VP's team members and thanked them over and over again. The employees cried, the team cried, and so did the VP.

I've been working on over-treatment for a long time and have written about it in The Treatment Trap, but this took my breath away. The opportunity cost is profound when it comes to transplants.

Medically unnecessary transplants take life away from those who could die without a new heart.[102]

Several months after I received this email, news reports revealed that the company paying for these second opinions for its employees was Walmart. Leah Binder, head of The Leapfrog Group (the health care quality improvement organization that releases hospital safety "grades")[103] interviewed Tom Emerick, a former Walmart VP in Forbes. Emerick told her about notes he'd received from Walmart employees, such as "Thank you for saving my husband's life" and "thank you for finding the right treatment for my daughter". She writes:

> *Exceptional doctors and nurses often get kudos like these from their patients routinely, but Tom is not a physician. Tom is just a good business leader. And it turns out, being "just a good business leader" is exactly the medicine our healthcare system needs.*
>
> *Walmart's move is smart, but rare. Many companies hesitate to recommend use of one hospital or another because they worry their employees will take a cynical view of their motives, and assume the purpose is purely to cut costs, not to save lives. Is it possible for employers to build enough trust among employees to credibly advise them on the highest performing hospitals?*
>
> *There is one way: by giving employees the information to decide for themselves. That means giving employees unfettered access to information on the safety and quality of care delivered at the hand-selected hospitals compared with every other hospital nationally … But going back to the larger issue, Walmart deserves credit for doing right by its employees. With transparency, its employees will know it.*[104]

Physician organizations are also taking steps to rein in the incidence of unnecessary medical tests and treatments, launching the "Choosing Wisely" campaign in early 2012. Sponsored by the ABIM (American Board of Internal Medicine) Foundation, it lays out a beautiful idea: that doctors embrace common sense in the practice of medicine. Each participating physician society (and there were nine at launch, representing 376,000 physicians) identifies five tests or procedures commonly used in their field, whose use should be discussed or questioned. For example, from the AAFF (American Academy of Family Physicians):

- Do not routinely prescribe antibiotics for acute mild-to-moderate sinusitis unless symptoms last for seven or more days or symptoms worsen after initial clinical improvement.
- Do not order electrocardiograms or other cardiac screening for low-risk patients without symptoms.

The lists came out in April 2012. A robust group of partner organizations including Consumer Reports is on board to help develop tools physicians can use to have these kinds of conversations with their patients. It's a good step, whose impact is hard to assess in these early stages.

"The Tsunami is Coming"

Accountable Care Organizations (ACOs) are also on target to change the dynamic of patient care. The initiative was created under the Affordable Care Act, signed into law in 2010 by President Obama. In this model, health plans contract with medical systems (a group of hospitals and physicians) to push high quality, less expensive treatment. The ACO takes responsibility for keeping enrollees out of costly hospitals and emergency rooms, working with them to manage medications and appointments. Providers divvy up any money saved with the health plan.

Unlike the HMOs of old, patients aren't restricted to certain groups of medical-care providers. Also the ACO is set up by providers, not an insurance company, so the doctors and hospitals can figure out their own system as long as it meets cost and quality targets. Many hire "care managers", such as nurses or social workers, who might call a patient at home to check on whether she's eating right, or visit the patient's home, looking for things like loose carpeting that can easily trip a frail patient, leading to a devastating fall.

Done right, this kind of care can achieve remarkable results. For years, CareMore, a company based in Cerritos, California, that operated twenty-six care centers across the Southwest (in 2011 it sold to WellPoint) had been using this approach with its 50,000 Medicare Advantage patients. It achieved a hospitalization rate 24 percent below average; hospital stays 38 percent shorter; and an amputation rate among diabetics 60 percent lower than average. "Perhaps most remarkable of all, these improved outcomes have come without increased total cost. Though they may seem expensive, CareMore's 'upstream' interventions—the wireless scales [where a patient's weight can be monitored remotely], the free rides to medical appointments, etc.—save money in the long run by preventing vastly more costly 'downstream' outcomes such as hospitalizations and surgeries. As a result, CareMore's overall member costs are actually 18 percent below the industry average."[105]

"[ACOs] will change the way we pay for health care," says Dr. Michael Cryer, national medical director for the employee benefits consultancy Aon Hewitt. "We are seeing the beginnings of a tsunami."[106]

The tsunami is building. By the end of 2012, ACOs were serving as many as 31 million patients, or roughly ten percent of the American population.[107] In January 2013, CMS announced another 106 had been signed up. Private insurers are expected to sign on in ever-greater numbers, as results start to come in, and to the extent they prove successful.

The glitch may come in how you define "successful". Writes Rosemary Gibson in *The Battle Over Healthcare*, "To whom will accountable care organizations be accountable? Most will be structured to profit their managers and doctors, not the public. Others will be created by good people who will design a system with the patient in mind. They will be few in number and smart patients will look for them.

"Like a game of musical chairs, no hospital wants to be left standing. Some hospital executives are using Accountable Care Organizations to create mega-institutions. Small, independent hospitals in urban and suburban areas will likely vanish…Oligopolies are accountable to no one and are free to roam like bullies at school. Health care reformers wanted to solve a problem, but they may have created a bigger one."[108]

Working in lockstep with ACOs is the Patient-Centered Medical Home (PCMH), where a primary physician leads and integrates all aspects of a patient's care throughout his or her lifetime. The patient is as an active participant and the family is involved, too. Though the concept dates back to the late 60's, federal grants became available to expand the model in 2011 as part of the Affordable Care Act.

Health care is everybody's business, and everyone should be looking for less expensive solutions. However, concepts like "cheaper" have historically had little resonance for patients, at least while insurance was picking up most of the bill. Like the proverbial frog cooking in a pot of water (where the heat is turned up so gradually it doesn't even realize it's being cooked until it's too late), it's hard to realize what the privilege of "not picking up the bill" costs us in our insurance premiums over the course of our working lives. David Goldhill lays it out with an example:

> Let's say you're a 22-year-old single employee at my company today, starting out at a $30,000 annual salary. Let's assume you'll get married in six years, support two children for 20 years, retire at 65, and die at 80. Now let's make a crazy assumption: insurance premiums, Medicare taxes and premiums, and out-of-pocket costs will grow no faster than your earnings—say, 3 percent a year. By the end of your working days, your annual salary will be up to $107,000. And over your lifetime, you and your employer together will have paid $1.77 million for your family's health care. $1.77 million! And that's only after assuming the taming of costs! In recent years, health care costs have actually grown 2 to 3 percent faster than the economy. If that continues, your 22-year-old self is looking at an additional $2 million or so in expenses over your lifetime— roughly $4 million in total…three-quarters of it spent by others on your behalf, deducted from your earnings before you received your paycheck. And that's a big reason why our health care system is so expensive.[109]

As more and more consumers find themselves with higher insurance co-pays, higher coverage deductibles, or having no insurance at all, the public outcry for price transparency gets louder. But finding out how much things cost—or even the rhyme or reason behind these fees—can leave you scratching your head.

"How Much Does That Cost?"

An *LA Times* article[110] on the wild variation on hospital fees offers examples: "Debbie Cassettari had outpatient foot surgery to remove a bone spur. She arrived at the surgery center at 8 a.m., left at 12:30 p.m., and the bill came to $37,000, not counting doctor fees…Gary Larson has a $5,000 deductible insurance plan but has found that his medical bills are cheaper if he claims he's uninsured and pays cash. Using that strategy, an MRI scan of his shoulder cost him $350. His brother-in-law went to a nearby clinic for an MRI scan of his shoulder, was billed $13,000, and had to come up with $2,500."

A *Pittsburgh Tribune-Review* article[111] exploring health care costs finds the price for identical medical procedures differs widely across the United States—not only by region, but even within the same hospital or clinic. Cost also depends on who pays—an insurer, Medicare, or you—and the differences can amount to thousands of dollars.

The newspaper found that hospitals, doctors, insurers, and the government cloak actual health care costs from the public through contractual agreements, often labeled as "proprietary," and through the use of complex reimbursement formulas. The system typically rewards providers with more money for ordering tests or performing procedures regardless of the cost—or sometimes the medical need.

Using publicly available Medicare data, studies of certain health care costs by private companies and nonprofit groups, and data obtained for some national health insurers, the report found:

- For the same magnetic resonance imaging (MRI) scan of the lower back, Aetna members could pay more than $3,100 in South Texas or less than $300 in South Florida. Uninsured patients could be charged more than $4,600.
- An MRI that costs Aetna members more than $1,300 at a hospital in Pittsburgh can be had for $425 at a Monroeville clinic.

- Unlike most states, Maine publishes the average cost of thirty common medical procedures online. The state's data show Anthem Blue Cross and Blue Shield HMO members can pay anywhere from $537 to $3,151 for a colonoscopy, depending on location. The insurer's PPO (Physician's Practice Organization) members pay from $559 to $4,526.

Differences in cost and quantity add up, especially at a time when federal lawmakers are looking for ways to slash the nation's budget deficit. The report says Medicare would have saved $41 billion per year from its annual budget of nearly $569 billion in fiscal year 2011 if all of its 306 hospital referral regions nationwide were limited to the lower beneficiary average in Minneapolis versus the Miami cost.

The federal government now mandates that restaurants publicly post nutrition information. Imagine if it mandated public disclosure of fees for medical procedures? Not only would this help us consumers learn and compare among providers, facilities, and procedures; it would allow us to add our voice to the body of public knowledge in online communities and through other means.

The marketplace isn't waiting for these projects to ramp up. Some examples:

Clearhealthcosts.com, a web platform currently in its beta phase (and starting with the state of New York), offers pricing information for medical procedures, gathering data from independent reporting, health care providers, participating consumers, and databases.

Medibid.com, an "eBay" for medical procedures launched in 2010, puts doctors together with patients who need care. The patient fills out a medical questionnaire and can upload their medical records (their identity is kept confidential until a transaction is consummated). MediBid-affiliated physicians and other medical providers respond by submitting competitive bids for the requested care.

In 2011 the company facilitated:

- More than fifty knee replacements, at an average price of about $12,000, almost one-third of what the insurance companies typically pay and about half of what Medicare pays.
- Sixty-six colonoscopies with an average price between $500 and $800, half of what you would ordinarily expect to pay.
- Forty-five knee and shoulder arthroscopic surgeries, with average prices between $4,000 and $5,000.

"Our goal," states the Medibid website, "is to provide the best opportunity for consumers to self-direct medical care."

Snaphealth.com, is an Amazon.com-like web platform where patients/consumers can search for a physician or procedure, make an appointment, and "save money by paying cash." Says co-founder David Wong, an ER physician, "People can make value-based decisions with real information." The first group in Snaphealth's sites: the uninsured.[112]

Castlighthealth.com is a startup offering employers, health plans, and consumers health care and cost transparencies that "lower the cost of providing health care benefits, while offering employees and plan members a consumer-friendly way to get the most for their out-of-pocket costs."

As resources like these become more robust, populated, and commonplace, consumerism will drive medical care to become more price and quality sensitive. The alternative is for tax-paying individuals to continue to be drained of resources all their working lives, only to face bankruptcy when a serious medical emergency arises.

To fully grasp the absurdity of our current third-party reimbursement system and the dysfunction it fosters, let's imagine (since we're talking about IKEA) a third party paid for our furniture. This third party would be contracted by our employers, or by our government. We wouldn't have much choice in this decision. Plus they'll tell us which stores we can shop in. Frankly, we're pretty relieved we don't have to pay the entire cost of the new sofa ourselves.

Though we'd have the option of checking out several stores, we'd find no price tags, feature descriptions, or warranties on anything. Questioning the staff would lead to looks of puzzlement and/or slight offense, with some vague response like "I'll make a note and see if the boss can get back to you." Attempts to compare the sofa, its features, or costs from store to store on the Internet would also prove frustrating. Most attempts to go beyond pretty pictures and broad statements would lead to dead ends.

We finally buy our sofa: it looks good, our friend recommended it, and we liked the staffer who showed it to us. We may have just spent a fortune, but we don't know; the full bill doesn't come to us. (That same bill may have been padded with "extras" of dubious value, but that's for the store and our third-party payer to worry about.) We'll never know if the simpler sofa next to the one we bought was just as good, or better. We grumble a bit about the co-pay, which is higher than we'd like, but after all, we thought we were getting "the best." And if we get the sofa home and find it's a horrible quality, we can't take it back; that's not part of the deal.

Worst case, the furniture collapses and hurts us. Then we find the furniture store will not share information about the specific model, manufacturer, distributor, or salesperson. We can try to hire a lawyer and sue; he will take one-third of any award. That's if he even takes the case at all. (Can you blame him? The chances of winning may be 20 % even with a good case, and the cost of bringing the case often exceeds damage award.) Meantime, that furniture store might be the only one around within a 100-mile radius; all our friends shop there, our children and the staff's children go to school together, and every Saturday we play golf with the VP of sales. Worse, people we care about, unaware of our bad experience, continue to buy what may be faulty, dangerous furniture from that same store. Ultimately, exhausted from months of legal depositions and depleted of energy, we are offered a financial settlement that will end the nightmare… on the condition we never tell anyone what really happened.

Meantime, the staffer who sold the sofa feels terrible that we got hurt. She knew there were problems with that model of sofa and had complained all the way up to her CEO. He may have made light of her concerns and made it clear her job depended on her silence. Though his salary is partly dependent on customer-satisfaction scores, it's more dependent on annual profit margin. The store's risk manager had assured him the payout to settle a few claims of collapsing sofas would be less than the cost of scrapping that entire line of sofas.

When all the dust settles, the furniture store and the manufacturer of the collapsing sofas are never forced to admit publicly that due to a cozy relationship with the supplier, they never tested the sofa to meet industry weight-bearing standards. Though they had to pony up a settlement to the injured, their revenues overall more than make up for it. The saleswoman leaves the business for another profession. The CEO celebrates an increase in salary and presides over the ribbon-cutting of a new wing of the sales floor. The third-party payer requests and obtains a rate increase, to cover the cost of these losses. It will simply pass these costs along to the customers' employers, who pay the third-party payers, who in turn pay for member furniture purchases.

This is a cynical caricature and huge oversimplification of the dysfunction in our health care system, but many will recognize truths in it. It speaks to the chasm that separates service and customer, a chasm that can only be brooked by disclosure, transparency, and, on the customer's side, engagement. As one observer notes, "If people paid for their cars with health insurance, everyone would be driving Mercedes."

Says David Goldhill:

Ten days after my father's death, the hospital sent my mother a copy of the bill for his five-week stay: $636,687.75. He was charged $11,590 per night for his ICU room; $7,407 per night for a semiprivate room before he was moved to the ICU; $145,432 for drugs; $41,696 for respiratory services. Even the most casual effort to compare these prices to marginal costs or to the costs of off-the-shelf components demonstrates the absurdity of these numbers, but why should my mother care? Her share of the bill was only $992; the balance, undoubtedly at some huge discount, was paid by Medicare.

Wasn't this an extraordinary benefit, a windfall return on American citizenship? Or at least some small relief for a distraught widow? Not really. You can feel grateful for the protection currently offered by Medicare (or by private insurance) only if you don't realize how much you truly spend to fund this system over your lifetime, and if you believe you're getting good care in return.

In the IKEA experience, customers know they are served by a cost structure reflective of a frugal and accountable culture. It's one that emanates from the core of its founder, a billionaire who still "opts to grocery shop in the afternoon when prices are lower, encourages IKEA employees to use both sides of paper when writing, and flies economy class."[113]

We go to IKEA to buy the equivalent of well-designed cheap cars, not Mercedes, knowing we can spend the savings on something else. The ethos of quality and frugality that drives furniture pieces into flat boxes, and the cost savings on to the consumer, deserves a place in the health care equation.

Imagine my father's hospital had to present the bill for his "care" not to a government bureaucracy, but to my grieving mother. Do you really believe that the hospital—forced to face the victim of its poor-quality service, forced to collect the bill from the real customer—wouldn't have figured out how to make its doctors wash their hands?

—**David Goldhill,** *"How American Health Care Killed My Father"*

MARK PRICES CLEARLY AND PAY BILLS OURSELVES:

Critical Opportunities for Health Care
1. **Respect parents' need to know the cost of tests and procedures.**

Critical Opportunities for Patients & Families
1. **Do your research on the websites such as those described above.**
2. **Ask "How Much is That?"**

7

If IKEA designed health care...

the team that serves us would act more team- like

For the secret of the care of the patient...is in caring for the patient.
—**Frances Peabody,** MD, 1927

In addition to chart-busting sales, IKEA boasts a slew of awards for how it does business. That includes *Business Week's* list of the "20 Best Companies for Leadership" (February 2010) as well as *Working Mother* magazine's annual list of the "100 Best Companies for Working Mothers," for four consecutive years. IKEA was listed on *Fast Company's* Fast 50 for its environmentally responsible products, as well as on *Training* magazine's annual list of top companies that excel at human capital development for five consecutive years. Since 2006, IKEA has been recognized by *Ethisphere* magazine as one of the World's Most Ethical companies.[114]

Behind its blue and yellow facade, the company is known for a democratic management structure, where no one is above the other in status. Few people in the company have titles, and no one, not even top executives, have an enclosed office.[115]

At IKEA's US headquarters building in Conshohocken, Pennsylvania, an open office plan is designed to encourage interaction. Says Nick O'Donnell, who oversaw the building's design, "Walls segregate people and keep them apart."[116]

Teamwork is valued at IKEA, and numerous glassed-in meeting rooms are intended to foster it. A 2008 doctoral thesis concluded that "IKEA employees' willingness to exchange knowledge is the single most important factor behind the company's global expansion, and that the participation of the employees in this process is crucial to the company's success."[117]

In December 2010, when a bleak economy saw many companies cutting back on or eliminating holiday gifts to employees, IKEA made headlines for stepping "out of the box." The company's holiday gift to all 12,400 US employees was a brand-new bike. The all-terrain bicycles, custom-built for IKEA, were meant to show "appreciation for employees' hard work—and offer an incentive for them to bike to work." (In true IKEA fashion, the bikes came in a flat box and needed to be assembled.)

IKEA recruited four hundred workers when it opened its first store in Belfast in 2007 and won an award for embracing diversity. The nonprofit that gave the award explains: "The company was keen for its new co-workers…to feel that their opinions were valued: IKEA's culture promotes realizing the potential of every individual and valuing everyone's diversity. They see this as an integral element of their competitive advantage."

> *Our workplaces are not for people with big egos. Togetherness is important. At IKEA, we can always get a helping hand from colleagues. We take responsibility, learn from our mistakes, and share our experience and knowledge with each other. That's how we grow together…*
>
> —*Welcome Inside,* an IKEA publication

IKEA workers are encouraged to share thoughts in open forums, and it has mandatory values workshops for managers and supervisors. Ensuring that diversity is celebrated is seen as an important aspect of the manager's job. So important that staff are asked to rate managers on this issue. Their score is incorporated into the salary review.

By contrast, teamwork and knowledge-sharing are hardly the hallmarks of most hospital structures. In fact, hierarchies in hospitals have practically been elevated to an art form. At the top of the food chain are doctors. Within the ranks of doctors themselves, there's a sub-food chain. On top are the senior physicians who make rounds on the floors once or twice a day. Next are the overworked residents, who essentially live in the hospital while training. At the bottom of the heap are medical students, who spend the most time with patients.[118]

Although some senior physicians welcome feedback from their juniors, others disdain it, either overtly or through intimidation. And students can be all too easily intimidated. In a 1993 article in *The New England Journal of Medicine,* a Harvard medical student reported that although her resident routinely made derisive remarks about her patients on rounds, the rest of the team laughed nervously rather than confront her.

Dr. Adam J. Wolfberg wrote a similar story in the same journal four years later. He reported that for years medical students performed pelvic examinations on anesthetized women who had not given consent—because senior obstetricians said it was the best way to learn internal anatomy. He says although this practice made many students uncomfortable, most were afraid to speak up.

Intimidation moves down the food chain from there. The Institute for Safe Medication Practices (ISMP), in a 2003 survey of more than two thousand health care providers, reported that physicians and other prescribers, pharmacists, nurses, and supervisors all engage in intimidating behaviors, such as using condescending language or voice intonation, expressing impatience with questions, displaying negative or threatening body language, reporting a staff member to his or her manager, and telling a nurse or pharmacist to "just give what was ordered."[119] Perhaps the most alarming finding, however, is that 7 percent of respondents reported being involved in a medication error in which intimidation contributed to the outcome.[120]

In decades of shadowing health care "team members" in several hospitals, observing how they interact, listening to their concerns, and writing several books about it, Suzanne Gordon sees a lack of what she calls "team intelligence", where workers may attend the same patients and work on the same unit but have never had training in communicating, respecting, consulting and trusting each other. Some may never have worked together before. In the hierarchal setting described above, it's a recipe for dysfunction, with the patient in the crosshairs. As Gordon writes in *First Do Less Harm: Confronting the Inconvenient Problems of Patient Safety* (Cornell University Press, 2012), "Pity the poor patient who is dependent on an intern who has not only been up for thirty hours, but also who has just been scolded by an attending during morning rounds for making a mistake (the kind of mistake that is essential to the learning process). Or the poor patient who is cared for by Dr. X and a nurse she has worked with for only a few days or even weeks. Or the new nurse whose RN colleagues are showing him who's boss on the unit. If teamwork is a matter of years spent earning the trust of higher-status professionals, patients will not be safe under the kinds of conditions that are all too common in health care—in which people work with people with whom they have never worked before."

It's often been suggested, as aviation and patient safety consultant John Nance alluded to earlier, that health care institutions could improve their safety record by adapting lessons from the aviation industry, which has made a science out of safety standards. (Checklists arose from this model.) One lesson is to get rid of the network of hierarchies. Airline crews, from a senior captain to a newly hired flight attendant, don't use formal titles when talking to each other in the cockpit, where safety is crucial and a slipup can lead to disaster. They address each other by first name only. This approach is believed to flatten the workplace hierarchy, creating a culture where co-workers feel comfortable enough to question each other, regardless of rank, if they believe something is amiss.

Contrast this with the culture at many hospitals, where nurses and other staff often address physicians by their titles and last names. This kind of traditional hospital hierarchy is notoriously intimidating, and it can have the dire consequence of making nurses or interns hesitant to challenge a doctor who may be ordering the wrong medicine or preparing to operate on the wrong site. There's a strong argument in health care that a first-name policy may contribute to a culture of safety, as it empowers medical staff, flattens hierarchies, and promotes teamwork. If we really value patient safety, even the most junior-level staff member should feel comfortable providing feedback, or sounding the alarm over a perceived hazard, without fear of a backlash.

Teamwork in health care is also compromised by front-line staff's lack of control over technologies, equipment and environments that may be untested, poorly designed, and/or prone to malfunction.

Consider "alarm fatigue". It's where the beeps from monitors attached to patients—designed to alert staff to potentially life-threatening conditions—become so relentless, and false alarms so numerous, that nurses become desensitized. A Boston Globe investigation found 200 patients died in a recent five-year period because nurses didn't hear or failed to react with urgency to beeping alarms. In March, 2012, a 17-year-old Pennsylvania girl died after a tonsillectomy; a powerful pain narcotic had stopped her breathing. The alarms hooked up to her had been muted, and a busy nurse didn't notice until it was too late.[121]

Writes Rosemary Gibson in *The Battle Over Healthcare*, "If nurses had a choice, they would refuse to work in hospitals where it is impossible to care for patients safely, but… [H]ospital executives often view nurses' concerns about safety as mere complaints." In a better world, end users of the products would be actively involved in decisions and trained in their use, something that rarely happens, says Gibson. "Equipment and device manufacturers take advantage of the knowledge vacuum and pitch an avalanche of new products as quick fixes to hospital executives. There is no quick fix…the solution is intelligent design of work to ensure safe care for every patient, every time."[122]

In the team hierarchy, the drug and device manufacturers that pitch this "avalanche of new products" are powerful forces. Writes Gibson, "Companies have been able to get away with poorly designed devices and equipment at immense human and financial cost. Hospitals don't hold product manufacturers accountable for product defects. In a stark contrast, it is inconceivable that Apple would tell its iPhone customers that it had plans to fix the glitch on the antenna 'in a few years'. This abysmal level of customer service is pervasive in the health care industry. Lobbyists for device manufacturers want fast-track approval. Government red tape stifles life-saving innovation, they say. With government out of the way, they can reach sales targets, yet another symptom of the pathological mutation that has gripped health care."[123]

Adding to the problem is this leaves the public in the dark about the truth. "The best evidence shows that half of all the clinical trials ever conducted and completed on the treatments in use today have never been published in academic journals", says physician Ben Goldacre, author of *Bad Pharma: How Drug Companies Mislead Doctors and Harm Patients.* "Trials with positive or flattering results, unsurprisingly, are about twice as likely to be published—and this is true for both academic research and industry studies. If I toss a coin, but hide the result every time it comes up tails, it looks as if I always throw heads. You wouldn't tolerate that if we were choosing who should go first in a game of pocket billiards, but in medicine, it's accepted as the norm."[124]

If staff occupies the nether regions of the hierarchy food chain, you can imagine where this leaves ill-informed and dependent patients. On the one hand, we don't know the whole truth about the efficacy of drugs and devices we put in our bodies. On the other, we worry that speaking up about things we feel are wrong risks antagonizing the people who hold our lives in their hands. When a patient does speak up to bad behavior, it can take courage and be quite effective. I applaud this woman's anonymous comment in response to an online news report about unsanitary conditions at a Canadian hospital:

> *When my hubby had surgery to remove his cancer, he was put in a semiprivate room, but three days later, he was moved into isolation because it was suspected he had C. difficile. On the door was a huge sign saying AFTER WASHING HANDS FOR 3 MINUTES, GOWNS, GLOVES, AND MASK REQUIRED BEFORE ENTRY. I did that and was sitting there talking to him, when three doctors walked in ... no water had been running, so they didn't wash their hands and none of them were wearing any of the items on the sign. A nurse walked by and pulled them out by their collars and showed them the sign, and they told her they didn't need that. I got up and stood in the doorway and told them that unless they did what I had to do, they weren't getting in, and they threatened to call security on me. I told them to*

try because my lawyer was on speed dial and I would have their kids, their houses, and pensions by the time I was finished. They left, and the nurse congratulated me. I used to be a nurse and doctors think they are gods and don't have to adhere to rules. WRONG!!!!!!

But far more patients are too intimidated to speak up, particularly older patients raised to bow to the physician's authority. And flattening hierarchies in this environment is a tough sell. As John Nance described earlier, the culture resists change. Peter Pronovost MD, a critical-care researcher at Johns Hopkins University, long a promoter of checklists proved to reduce infections and medical errors, clearly finds this frustrating. In his book *Safe Patients, Smart Hospitals: How One Doctor's Checklist Can Help Us Change Health Care from the Inside Out*, he writes:

Why isn't hand washing standardized in hospitals—along with thousands of other procedures that are known to save lives? It would be easy to blame doctors, but the bulk of the problem does not lie there. Most physicians care deeply about their work and want nothing but the safest care for their patients. It's the culture of medicine and the systems within which doctors practice that are at fault. Physicians, including myself, are trained to believe that we don't need standardization because we don't make mistakes; we are told that our brains have endless storage capacity and that we have perfect recall of all the thousands of hours of information we've learned from medical school and years of practice. Yet we do not. The fact is, just like all other humans, we forget. We are fallible. We do not see systems and we are not trained to improve them.

Furthermore, doctors are also trained to believe that we don't always have to follow the rules or ask for anyone's help. We are the smartest people in the world and can figure out any problem on our own. When I was in medical school, I remember specifically being told, "Guidelines are for simple physicians, not Hopkins physicians. At Hopkins we know the evidence, we are expert clinicians; we know the nuances of our patients so we do not need guidelines." I have since realized how dangerous it is to use that statement to train physicians…

As science continues to propel us into the future at an alarming rate, the culture of medicine dwells solemnly in the past. We do not train clinicians about the value of standardization, we do not train physicians to share knowledge or to improve bad systems that harm patients, we do not train physicians to work as a team organized around the patient, and for the most part we do not hold them accountable for their performance, or patient outcomes.

"The Silence Was Deafening"

Dale Micalizzi lives with the terrible fallout from this attitude. Her eleven-year-old son Justin entered the hospital to have an infected ankle drained. During surgery his heart stopped, and his lungs began hemorrhaging from the breathing tube.

Below is the letter she sent to his surgical team and posted on her blog, justinhope.tumblr.com.

The letter that took me ten years to write...
September 11, 2011
Dear Anesthesiologist, Orthopedic Surgeons, and Hospital CEO (names removed from this post):
You may remember our youngest child, Justin. He was eleven. You cared for him ten years ago. He presented to you on Jan. 15, 2001 for an incision and drainage of a septic ankle.
We believe that the surgery was performed (primarily by the orthopedic resident) during which time Justin experienced a series of cardiac arrests accompanied by a pulmonary hemorrhage from the endotracheal tube. He was transported to the PICU [pediatric intensive care unit] at another facility (name removed from post) in grave condition and died that next morning after being removed from life support with no hope of survival. His brother and sister were asked by the chaplains to be present to say goodbye. Being teenagers at the time, this was a life-changing and difficult journey for them and his entire family, his friends, and his community. Traumatic, unexpected loss and grief are the most unbearable.

Upon our arrival home, the coroner's office called, stating that "something was not right" and that we should seek an attorney.

With the help of a cardiothoracic surgeon, we retained an attorney to help us find answers. Litigation was chosen because the multiple attempts to speak with you honestly about the care that our son received from you were not taken seriously. The silence was deafening. Although deaths may be common occurrences for physicians, they are not for parents. Children are more than blood and bones. If you have children, you are aware of this. Parents need more than a simple answer of "we have no idea" when their child dies. The better option for all of you in the future may be to tell parents, "We have no idea what happened, but we will do everything in our power to find out."

You may remember the depositions. We attended all of those meetings and listened carefully to your words as we remembered every detail prior to the OR. You may not know that I was also questioned for approximately seven hours about the care of my son leading up to this event. I must tell you that, although my attorney said that a mother has never been more prepared and caring, I found that experience to be cruel and inhumane. I did nothing wrong and I loved my son more than words can explain. As I learned from my visit to professors at a NY law school, questioning the parent to such an extent was simply a tactic, albeit inhumane, to have the case dropped.

Listening to your heart instead of your attorney's jargon may have been a better option for all of us. I refuse to believe that physicians are lacking, to this degree, in humanity, which is why I continue to work with them. It is difficult to face a parent after a child dies in your care, but it is a responsibility that comes with the territory.

I have worked tirelessly for the past ten years trying to promote pediatric patient safety and transparency in medicine. On this quest, I have had the pleasure of working with some of the most brilliant of national health care leaders and many anesthesiologists and surgeons. Because of these connections, I am allowed behind the scenes of health care that most parents or patients would never see. They trust me.

I received a call from one of these physicians recently: nine years, nine months, and four days after our son's death. He said that a colleague of yours stated that he couldn't live with himself any longer, knowing that I was still searching for the truth. He went on to say that all of you, and your attorneys, knew from the beginning that Justin was overdosed on Phenylephrine. He said that the physician had reached for the wrong medication in error and used it in overdose proportions. I shared this new information with all of the physicians that have helped me over the years. Learning from the event is important to me. My child did not die in vain.

...Although this physician informant's information was troubling, it was also healing. You see, parents blame themselves when something happens to their child. It was our duty to keep him safe. You may not understand this, but I could literally feel the burden of the unknown melting from my shoulders, even though I have yet to hear the rest of the story. Justin was our child and I am grateful to the physician who finally had the courage to tell me a bit of the truth.

Forgiving you for withholding this information from me and my family has been difficult. I will never forget the events of that day or following, but I am getting closer to accepting the truth as an error or an accident that was poorly handled. I never believed that anyone meant to harm Justin.

My hope would be that fear of litigation will not prompt you to repeat these poor choices if tragedy should strike another family in your care. Your patients deserve better. We trusted you to tell the truth and to do your best. Perhaps, someday you will be able to share Justin's story with your students so that they can learn from your mistakes and another child's life can be saved.

Most Sincerely,

Dale Ann Micalizzi, Founder/Director

Justin's HOPE at The Task Force for Global Health

Around the same time she sent this letter, ten years after her son died, imagine how horrified Dale was to find herself in the emergency room again, this time with her husband, who was doubled over in pain (he'd been sent home after a prior check on this same pain, ten days before).

Dale's conversation with the anesthesiologist prior to gall-bladder surgery, and what happened next, is chilling. Incredibly she was also unable to head off what nearly became a second tragedy for her family. She shares the story in hopes physicians will read her words and want to do better for patients and families.

I asked to speak with the anesthesiologist before surgery. I [figured I] could use the patient/family anesthesia checklist that I had created with Dr. Henry Rosenberg right about then. I tried to remember the steps...what do I ask and what do I tell? I told Justin's story to the anesthesiologist who was going to be using one of the meds that I don't quite trust, Succinylcholine. It is a triggering agent for those that may have a genetic predisposition.

The anesthesiologist told me authoritatively, "Do not tell that story about your son again, as it is upsetting to anesthesiologists." I said, "Excuse me, but that is our family history and you must know what we know about what happened to our son." Geez, I thought to myself... nothing has changed in ten years. They still don't listen or think we know anything. He said that docs have to weigh things when they give anesthesia and his best option was to use the sux; so he did. His behavior in this situation touches on arrogance...

The gallbladder was removed, which took several hours because it was very near a gangrenous state and had to be ruptured in order to remove it as it was wrapped around organs. The surgeon said that it was a mess. Irrigation was completed. They removed it twelve hours after we arrived at the ED (after being "bumped" twice). But there was still some kind of blockage that seemed to be obstructing the bile duct...my husband needed a [procedure] which feeds a tube down his throat to make sure of what the blockage was to the bile duct. I later learned that this specific procedure was risky and highly litigious due to complications and errors.

The gastroenterologist arrives later that morning, and we also tell him Justin's story, and he said that no one has ever died in his care except once, and "that was the surgeon's fault," he whispers. He has done colonoscopies for years and he would basically use the same meds that he uses for those. My husband says, "I don't want to be your second patient to die." They laugh…

Now the family starts to arrive. My daughter is with me outside the gastro suite where we could hear what was happening quite clearly. Several minutes later, the dreaded "Call a code!" is screamed and confusion erupts. My daughter and I look at each other and freeze. Not again! The surgeon runs in along with a slew of docs…and the dreaded clergy. We knew what that meant. I grab the garbage can as nausea is now setting in as before…

The gastro doc enters the waiting room saying, "I'm really a good doctor, you know." More confusion…the nurse yells, "He's still not waking up." We hear, "Reverse the meds." The gastro doc runs back in.

Within minutes the surgeon comes out and said, "He's OK," and holds my hand, which I clenched for dear life as the crowd of physicians surrounded us…

If a patient and family member tells you that their child or loved one has died during anesthesia previously, could you please listen to them when they tell you to be careful? Don't blow them off, saying that the incident was a fluke or the other family member had an incompetent anesthesiologist or that you know what you're doing. Please do a little extra for that family so they don't have to experience a code again. Yes, we know it could happen again, but if you listen, perhaps we could prevent it together…

I offered my services to the hospital's quality and safety dept. and completed an honest survey with no response from the hospital. I'm quite good at analyzing safety now. Perhaps you can learn from a patient and family who have experienced a personal medical tragedy, as they can help you do better. Don't be afraid of them or think they know nothing. They want to help and most are kind.

The rest of the story was uneventful and my husband has completely recovered. The surgeon and nurses were terrific. Thank you for saving my husband, I said, as I hugged them! Yes, I even hugged the gastro doc that I was told by everyone (including my ninety-one-year-old mom and her friends later) had no bedside manner and was abusive to *the nurses. Maybe my hug changed him and the incident softened his perceived arrogance…or maybe not…*

What mattered most was that my husband was OK. We didn't have to bring home the dreaded bag of belongings…which crossed our minds immediately. So we were thankful that we would all be together for Thanksgiving.

Safety and communication has improved since Justin died eleven years ago to some extent, but there is still so much more to learn and do.

Turning Harm into Healing

On November 18, 1999, Linda Kenney, a wife and mother of three young children, went into a prominent Boston hospital for ankle surgery. Anesthesia was administered to block feeling from the knee down. Within minutes, she had a grand mal seizure and went into full cardiac arrest. Her heart could not be re-started. The surgical team wheeled her across the hall, cut her chest open, and put her on a cardio-pulmonary bypass machine.

Linda woke up three days later in the ICU. She was in the hospital ten days.

And nobody talked about what had happened.

What had happened was that the nerve block administered to her ankle had accidentally entered her blood. It quickly hit her heart, which was promptly anesthetized and stopped pumping.

Linda was grateful to be alive. It would be awhile before she could emotionally process what had happened. Her family was traumatized.

So, as it turns out, was her anesthesiologist, Rick van Pelt. He sent her a letter (without hospital permission), in which he apologized for what had happened, said he would make himself available any time she needed him, and signed it with his contact information, including his home phone number.

Months later they met, and started talking.

"I felt compelled to change the system which had failed me," she writes in the website of the organization she founded. "I experienced an incredible sense of responsibility because I was one of the lucky ones to have survived. I came to know first hand that there was a large hole in the healthcare system which needed to be filled."

Linda went on to found MITSS (Medically Induced Trauma Support Services) "to create awareness and educate patients, families, and the healthcare community about the emotional impact following adverse events". MITSS offers counseling and support to both patients—and providers—following adverse events. Today, MITSS' annual November fundraising dinner brings 500 supporters from all over the country, with the majority of sponsors hospital and health systems. I've attended for the last several years. For me, one person who's experienced medical harm in my family, I find it healing and illuminating to hear how these events impact people on the *other* side.

Among other things, Linda's success proves what one person can accomplish with vision, tenacity hard work, and focusing on the greater good—all very "team-like" attributes.

Nine years after Linda coded in the OR, Michelle Malizzo Ballog was wheeled into surgery at University of Illinois Hospital in Chicago. Doctors were going to replace a temporary stent in her liver. She was nervous, and with good reason: in a procedure two weeks earlier at the same hospital, she'd awakened too early from the anesthesia.

But this time, she never woke up. A 39-year-old mother of two young children, Michelle would die nine days after surgery.

Her parents' grief, shock and anger were overwhelming. But in the events that followed, Bob and Barb Malizzo were empowered to find some purpose in their pain. They, like Linda, created a legacy for others, teaming with the hospital to show how an adverse event can be handled "the right way".[125]

It began with disclosure. When the Malizzos met with Chief Safety officer Timothy McDonald a few days after the surgery, their daughter was on life support. The Malizzos expected McDonald to blame "anyone but the hospital" for their daughter's death. But instead of dodging questions or referring them to the hospital's lawyers, McDonald told them he'd find out what had happened. Days later he shared with them results of an internal investigation: clinicians supervising the operation failed to notice that Michelle had stopped breathing during the surgery. She'd been over-anesthetized, and had suffered massive brain injury from the subsequent loss of oxygen.

McDonald apologized, promised to stay accessible to the Malizzos in the days ahead, and quickly offered a settlement to provide for Michelle's two daughters, who were 1 and 7 at the time.

The Malizzos could have hired a lawyer, filed a lawsuit, and pursued a massive payout after years of costly litigation. Instead, they say their goal was to make sure what happened to their daughter didn't happen to anyone else.

The hospital changed its process for giving anesthesia to make it safer. A second change took longer: it was a year before the Malizzos had worked through their grief enough to accept McDonald's invitation to serve on the UIC Medical Center's patient safety committee. Today, they drive 90 minutes from their home in Hobart Indiana to attend monthly committee meetings. They're briefed beforehand about whatever facts and medical background will help them provide meaningful input. "We talk about hospital errors not only at UIC but also errors at other hospitals or harm that was done to people at other hospitals," Malizzo says. "We check our policies and procedures at UIC and if we see they are deficient, we make the changes to prevent some kind of error from occurring. So we review not only potential errors that happen at UIC but errors at other hospitals as well."[126]

The process, called "Seven Pillars", is based on openness about medical errors or near-misses so health care providers can fix and prevent them. It was adopted by the Chicago hospital system in 2006. Today, it's getting attention from hospitals in other states. (A similar program at the University of Michigan has cut costs per claim in half since 2001.) [127]

Seven Pillars include these steps:

- Report incidents that could harm patients.
- Investigate those cases and fix problems before an error happens.
- Communicate when an error occurs, even if no harm was done.

- Apologize and "make it right" by waiving hospital and doctors' fees.
- Fix gaps in the system that can cause things to go wrong.
- Track data from patient safety reports and see if changes make things safer.
- Educate and train staff how to make care safer.

In the two years since it started, the process led to more than 100 investigations and nearly 200 specific improvements. It was also the basis for twenty full disclosures of inappropriate care that caused patient harm. The Agency for Healthcare Research and Quality (AHRQ) is currently funding a three-year project to expand the Seven Pillars' success in ten Chicago-area hospitals.

McDonald is also coaching hospital systems outside of Illinois on using the Seven Pillars. As he travels the country, he brings Bob and Barb Malizzo—"they're part of the team", he says—to tell their story. The audience is frequently moved to tears and a standing ovation.

Mistakes Happen

Let's agree good teams are built in part by analyzing mistakes and learning to overcome them.

Now imagine you're a doctor who's made an honest mistake, and someone died because of it. You're wracked by guilt and an urge to apologize. But the hospital insists you don't talk to the victim.

In a culture where mistakes are not allowed, they can't exist. What doesn't exist can't be talked about. Living with the resulting guilt, pain and shame, as we saw in the case of Linda Kenney's anesthesiologist, brings its own brand of devastation.

"Let's talk about mistakes", said Brian Goldman from the stage during his TED Talk presentation in November 2011. Goldman, a Canadian Emergency Room doctor, proceeded to describe to the audience an experience he'd had as a young physician. He'd missed a sign of trouble, one that ultimately resulted in the death of a woman who was also a mother and grandmother. "Over the next few weeks, I beat myself up and I experienced for the first time the unhealthy shame that exists in our culture of medicine—where I felt alone, isolated, not feeling the healthy kind of shame that you feel, because you can't talk about it with your colleagues." For a time afterward Goldman questioned his choice of profession. Then, after he'd recovered, he describes in his talk how he made another mistake... and then another. (Though fortunately they were caught by colleagues before harm resulted). "And I'd like to be able to say to you that my worst mistakes only happened in the first five years of practice as many of my colleagues say, which is total B.S." (the crowd laughs at the absurdity). "Some of my doozies have been in the last five years. Alone, ashamed and unsupported. Here's the problem: If I can't come clean and talk about my mistakes ... how can I teach [my colleagues} about what I did so that they don't do the same thing?" Goldman says mistakes are inevitable. "So if you take the system, as I was taught, and weed out all the error-prone health professionals, well, there won't be anybody left."[126]

Was Goldman booed off the stage after admitting that all doctors make mistakes?

In fact, he got a standing ovation. "I felt freer and lighter than I had felt for years," he wrote in the Huffington Post. "I could stand on a clear, sunny day, say that I'm human, and not worry about being asked to leave the room." A year after his TED Talk was posted, it had nearly 700,000 views. He writes that an equal if not greater number have shared it on Facebook and other social networking sites.

"I've been buoyed by the hundreds of comments I've received. A small number of people have (rightly) taken me to task for not doing better. Some tried to show me how I could have prevented the medical mistakes to which I confessed. But most have been incredibly supportive of my call for health professionals to talk openly about their mistakes."

Weeding Out "Bad Apples"

Peter Pronovost is doubtlessly right that "most physicians care deeply about their work and want nothing but the safest care for their patients." I've been privileged to meet many myself, and it's thanks to their skill and knowledge that some of the people dearest to me are alive today. However as in any profession, there are bad apples—and the profession would do well to weed them out.

For patients, it's almost impossible to know beforehand just who these bad apples are. A doctor who's been sanctioned for egregious behavior by the medical board in one state sometimes simply moves to another and sets up practice there. For example, in 2005, a Suffolk County (Massachusetts) jury decided that Dr. Mary Ames-Castro and another obstetrician caused irreversible brain damage to an infant girl during a delivery at Massachusetts General Hospital. The $23.8-million malpractice judgment was one of the largest in state history. But the judgment was never entered in a public database maintained by the state Board of Registration in Medicine. The board erased Ames-Castro's profile from the database because she let her license expire after the botched procedure.

As of January 2013, she is licensed to practice in both Oregon and Wisconsin under her maiden name, Mary Beth Ames. Because neither Oregon nor Wisconsin publicly records out-of-state malpractice judgments—and because Massachusetts deleted Ames-Castro's profile— her current patients are left with the false impression that their doctor has a clean record.

Hospital administrators will also tell you "weeding out the bad apples" is harder than you think. Rick Boothman, chief risk officer for the University of Michigan Health System,[129] says dealing internally and responsibly with a physician's bad behavior can be a challenge, even when "everyone knows who they are." Boothman talks of a surgeon who told him recently:

"'I was on faculty here six months, at only six months I could give you a short list of people I never wanted to be in an operating room with.'" In such cases, says Boothman, "…interestingly, getting the names is hard. In that conversation I slid a legal pad across the table and I said, 'Write them down and I'll start looking at them,' and he wouldn't write them down.

"There's a complex question about what to do next. First with the culture change: peer review, for instance, has traditionally meant that we wait until somebody bottoms out, until someone has become such an embarrassment or so utterly unsafe that we can't ignore it anymore, then we pluck them out and engage in a very messy and risky process of pulling their privileges or submitting them to a licensing board. That's our shame.

"We need to get out in front of these people before they become an embarrassment and before they hurt a lot of people. So we're doing a number of things here that are very exciting." Boothman turns peer review into an approach that is embracing, instead of disciplinary. "We [enroll] them in various programs to help them with communication skills or understand why they're challenged…[we] sample the residents quarterly in an anonymous way and just ask them, 'What's on your mind? What are you worried about? Who are you worried about? … So sampling patients, sampling residents, sampling the nursing staff—you go to a floor and just ask, 'What keeps you up at night?'[130]

Philip Levitt, MD, says it's time for a more direct approach. He points the finger of blame for medical harm and death squarely at bad doctors.[131] (Copyright privileges require the article be printed in its entirety.)

This is a commentary about health care. It tells why we are losing the battle to prevent over 100,000 unnecessary deaths in America's hospitals each year. My opinion is that physicians are primarily responsible for the deaths. A recent poll of Swedish doctors showed that a sizable minority felt that physicians were the source of most patient mishaps. That doesn't prove anything, of course. But I will stand by the facts in the body of my commentary below.

I'm a retired neurosurgeon who served as a chief of staff and governing board member of two separate 400-bed community hospitals over a five-year period. I learned where most of the skeletons were hidden. I was a reformer who tried to remove doctors who repeatedly hurt their patients. There were several of them at each hospital. Their sins included refusing to show up in an emergency, lying to patients and other doctors, missing diagnoses, getting poor operative results, doing unnecessary surgeries, and extracting sexual favors from patients. My efforts were opposed by my colleagues, the hospital administrators, and the hospital lawyers. I sensed that protecting bad doctors was a significant cause of the unnecessary loss of 98,000 lives a year from harmful adverse events. To Err is Human, a book by the Institute of Medicine, revealed that stark figure to a shocked public in 2000.

I had to do some lifting and probing before I could turn my intuition into arguments. My research into why my experience was nearly universal led me to someone who mined the National Practitioner Data Bank, Dr. Robert Oshel, who worked for the data bank before he retired. That repository was established by Congress in 1986 and put into effect at the end of 1990. It lists for the public, by a number only, those physicians who have been sued successfully or have lost their license to practice. Here's what he found over a period of twenty years:

- *There is a hard core of 2 percent of the physicians whose misdeeds result in half of the money paid out in malpractice cases.*
- *The average hospital drops only one doctor from its staff every twenty years.*
- *About 250 doctors lose their licenses each year, or 0.04 percent of the total. At that rate it would take fifty years to remove the hard-core 2 percent from practice.[132]*

There is an insidious cause of undue leniency to doctors who repeatedly hurt patients in To Err is Human *itself. The authors had turned the interpretation of the original data of their own published findings, the Harvard Medical Practice Studies, their primary source, on its head based on theoretical, not empirical grounds. No new studies were done so that no new data were gathered to contradict the original. The original numbers showed that at least 61 percent of adverse events in hospitals were the result of blunders by individual physicians and that systems errors were responsible for only 6 percent. I questioned the chief author of both studies, Dr. Lucian Leape of Harvard, in a series of e-mails, and found his explanations for his monumental reversal inadequate and unscientific.[133]*

To Err Is Human *had famously blamed bad health care delivery systems, not bad doctors. It emphasized "creating safety systems inside health care organizations through the implementation of safe practices at the delivery level. This level is the ultimate target of all the recommendations." As a result, all of the efforts to save the lives of the 98,000 per year have been systems based. The licensing boards of all the states, the main bulwarks against bad doctors, have bought into this and made a joint statement to that effect in 2008. They said, "Systemic sources of risk significantly eclipse professional incompetence as the dominant cause of harm to patients." The evidence from the Harvard Medical Practice Studies was otherwise.*

Documentation that the systems correction approach was not working came in two devastating reports that came out in November 2010, one from the Inspector General of HHS, based on data gathered on Medicare patients, and the other from Harvard Medical School based on outcomes in several North Carolina hospitals. That state was chosen because its hospitals had the reputation of rigorously following systems-error prevention methods. Both reports said that in the first decade of this century, the period following the publication of To Err is Human, *the number of deaths from adverse events was unchanged from the fifteen years preceding, perhaps greater, and had stalled at 120,000 per year. According to the facts, we are getting almost nowhere in our efforts to reduce hospital mishaps.*

It boils down to this: The most reasonable interpretation of the Harvard Medical Practice Studies is that the greatest share of responsibility for harmful errors falls on individual physicians, not bad systems. The systems approach, while it was a huge and rapid success in preventing airline mishaps and poorly manufactured cars, has made only a small dent in the number of unnecessary deaths in American hospitals. That tiny inroad came in avoiding three to six thousand deaths a year from infected intravenous lines, thanks to Dr. Peter Pronovost of Hopkins, an accomplishment which got swallowed up by the number of deaths from other sources. Over a million will die in the next decade. We have no time to lose. We must rid the profession of repeatedly erring doctors on a much larger scale than the minute fraction that we remove now.

Boothman responds, "The absence of accountability, whether an injury results directly from a personal mistake or a 'systems failure' has been a serious reason why we haven't improved over the years, in my opinion." However, he adds, "...there is plenty of blame to go around. It's naïve to suggest that only 2 percent of the doctors create the problem if for no other reason than the reality: those doctors do NOT practice in a vacuum. The hospital administrator or CEO who looks the other way when a doctor bills a lot or cuts corners is just as blameworthy as the doctor himself."[134]

What can a CEO do to make physicians accountable for harming patients? It's not so simple, say Drs. Robert Wachter and Peter Pronovost: "In American hospitals...physicians have traditionally been individual entrepreneurs, not employees, and thus are subject only to weak peer enforcement through medical staff structures. Not only do peers often recoil from disciplining 'one of our own,' but hospitals have been reluctant to punish physicians for fear of alienating them and losing the business they bring in."[135]

Wachter and Pronovost go on to suggest penalties for selected transgressions, once initial warnings and counseling have failed. For instance, not practicing hand hygiene would result in "education and loss of patient-care privileges for one week." Failure to perform a time-out before surgery would lead to "education and a two-week loss of operating room privileges."

"Until now," say Wachter and Pronovost, "we have shuffled this issue to the bottom of the deck, preferring to work on easier, less contentious safety activities, such as computerization and checklists. It is time to raise this topic to the top of our agenda. Having our own profession unblinkingly deem some behaviors as unacceptable, with clear consequences, will serve as a vivid example of our professionalism and thus represent our best protection against...outside intrusions [e.g. regulators and legislators]. But the main reason to find the right balance between 'no blame' and individual accountability is that doing so will save lives."

Adds Boothman, "We serve a health care community that is only now in the earliest stages of culture change from physician-centricity to patient-centricity, and we have a long way to go to get past the slogans and really design a system—*and a culture*—that truly puts the patient's interests at the center of all we do."

GETTING THE TEAM TO ACT MORE TEAM-LIKE

Critical Opportunities for Healthcare

1. **Create a shared value proposition** for all administrators, doctors and nurses on patient-centered care (like IKEA's mandatory values workshops)
2. **Transform peer review approach** into embracing rather than disciplinary model (Anonymous opinion sampling)
3. **Define and enforce penalties** for selected transgressions, including mandatory enrollment in programs targeted for specific behaviors.
4. **Implement monthly 'open forums'** for caregivers to share their concerns with each other and brainstorm solutions.

Critical Opportunities for Patients & Families

1. **Model the civility and respect** you'd like to see from your care providers. Make friends. Enlist someone on your care team to be your ally. Never underestimate the power of being nice.
2. **After discharge, write or email the hospital CEO** to commend good teamwork, or with suggestions about how it might be improved.

8

If IKEA designed health care...

hackers (the good kind) would thrive

Hacker [hak'-er] *n: A person who makes innovative customizations or combinations of retail electronic and computer equipment.*

Health care hacker (for good) *n: A person with a singular, "outlier" vision of how to look at "the way it's always been done," and achieves something better.*

Some people look at a shoe rack at IKEA and see a shoe rack. Some look at a shoe rack and see a tiered audio storage system. When Michael F. Zbyszynski saw two red salad bowls, he saw a speaker array. "It's all about not accepting what's presented for sale as it is," says Michael, "about not just doing a 'paint by numbers' of your life."

Salad-bowl speakers, countertops merged into room dividers, ottomans made into coffee tables—these are the works of "IKEA hackers." They view IKEA's products as raw materials and share their "re-inventions" at www. ikeahacker.blogspot.com.

Though IKEA cautions people not to change the function of furniture to risk safety, it embraces the hackers. Mona Liss, IKEA's PR director, attributes the trend to "this invisible aura of IKEA, something in our DNA that is inviting and unspoken," adding, "we're a culture that's asked to challenge conformity, to speak outside the box."[136]

Challenging conformity—not blindly accepting how things like politics, practices, and protocols are "packaged" for our consumption—is healthy. And no more so than in health care. So when I use the phrase "health care hackers" to describe some fascinating people who are thinking "outside the box" and showing us a different way, it's with only the utmost admiration. One such person, who lives on a tiny island off the coast of Italy, focuses on staying healthy on the inside; another, who lives in a designer home on a mountaintop north of Denver, focuses more on the physical environment. A third, whom you've been introduced to already, doesn't want you to have to "hack together" your own products—he knows how desperate you'll be for the right device some day, and is working to get better choices on store shelves. All are mavericks in the best possible way.

Healing with Food

Peter Lambert, who served for many years as personal chef to an elite client list including Robert Wood Johnson IV (yes, that one), saved his wife Amy from a potential lifetime of chronic illness, or worse. You may recall from the introduction to this book that Amy contracted a *C. diff* infection while in a New York City hospital for the birth of their daughter and was desperately ill. Long a believer in the power of food and the natural world to keep bodily functions in balance, her husband Peter called upon this approach to "cure" the disease that nearly claimed his wife's life—or, as he describes it, to restore the normal balance in the colon. She writes:

> *We were both committed to staying away from the antibiotics as a form of treatment. It didn't take a genius to figure out that antibiotic-induced colitis can't be effectively eliminated with antibiotics. In fact, the more we read about C. diff, the more we heard about people who were on a constant roller coaster of acute illness, antibiotics, remission, and start again six weeks later. They would take the course of Flagyll*

or Vancomycin, end the course, feel better, and then the new hatch [C. diff spores] would occur, and they would feel sick again and have to begin another course of antibiotics. This is no way to live. I felt OK about ten days into our protocol. Not good. Definitely not well. But not horrible. Then Peter came across a lone reference to C. diff in AIDS patients and the use of a probiotic called saccheromyces boulardii.

The day I began the saccheromyces boulardii, I knew that I was going to live; I knew that I was going to be really fine. I didn't know how long it would take, but I knew I would eventually get there. We used Jarrow Formulas Saccheromyces Boulardii + MOS. Most probiotics, we learned, don't ever make it to the colon. They don't weather the acidity of the stomach. Saccheromyces boulardii is specific to the colon. It may be exactly what was wiped out in my large intestine between the two rounds of castor oil to induce labor and the Clindamycin, an antibiotic that has been absolutely linked to C. diff. Saccheromyces is a yeast, not a bacteria. It made a huge difference in my mood, in the frequency of bouts of diarrhea, and in my overall energy.

A couple of days later we had an appointment to see an MD associated with [a prominent northeast hospital] who also had a background in homeopathy. He had seen our midwife's other client and was becoming an accidental alternative expert on C. diff. He listened to our protocol and was impressed. He shook our hands, commended Peter on his research and wisdom, and then handed me his card with his e-mail address. "When you need the antibiotics, just shoot me an e-mail. You don't even have to come in." I explained that I had turned the corner and that I really felt like it was over. He smiled and said, "This is going to be a war that will last months, if not years. I am happy you feel better today, but you will need to take the antibiotics eventually." I don't remember his name. Surely he doesn't remember mine. He was wrong. And I knew it then…

What is most unfortunate is that he never bothered to write down what we did, the protocol that Peter developed, and he never found out that I didn't eventually need the drugs. He is probably still telling C. diff sufferers to use the standard anti-diarrhea homeopathic remedy, rendered useless by the accompanying prescription for Vancomycin,

thereby initiating a long drawn-out war between bug and drug in the battleground of a damaged colon. It doesn't have to be this way.
It has been over five years since I contracted C. diff during my hospital stay…I have avoided writing our story because it is a reminder of how scary that time was. Rather than it being a time of joy and celebration, I perceive it as a period of weakness and failure, but I think that is partially the bug that does that. It sucks the life force, and hope, from you. The good news is that it all turned out okay. For us.
I hope that our story will help others to believe in the power of natural health care options and to trust in their own intuition.

—**Amy Burke**, Doctor of Chiropractic,
as told to the Peggy Lillis Foundation

When I e-mailed Amy for permission to share her story, I wasn't even sure the message would reach her. She and Peter, and their now six-year-old daughter, had moved from New York City to Pantelleria, a tiny, windswept island off the coast of Sicily. Not only did Amy give permission, she suggested I speak with her husband, initially because she read my reference to bleach being the best product to kill *C. diff* spores, and told me he had some thoughts to share. We arranged a Skype date and I went to their blog, flourishnourishinpantelleria.blogspot.com, to learn more about them. I was intrigued by their move and the business they set out to create on Pantelleria: "Our goal is to facilitate a wellness experience in which fresh air, amazing fresh food from the island and surrounding areas, geothermal waters, the Mediterranean Sea, the gentle and balanced pace of Italian living, and chiropractic will provide a vacation unlike anything you've yet to experience."

A few days later, through the miracle of technology, I found myself engaged in what turned into a two-hour conversation with a fascinating man. We began by talking about using bleach to eliminate *C. diff* from surfaces in hospitals and nursing homes. Lambert told me that a much more effective product is hydrogen peroxide, which is not corrosive, has no harsh fumes, and breaks down into simple hydrogen and water. He sent me a link to a study published by the National Institute of Health showing that, indeed, it appears to be nearly twice as effective.[137]

Lambert's true passion and expertise center on how food, wellness, and state of mind are so intertwined. As Amy had written, Peter is "a chef by training, a researcher by passion, and a natural-remedies sage by demand." In developing his expertise, Peter hacks together his degree from the American Culinary Institute, the perspective of the many physicians and scientists in his family, years of real-life experience, and a respect for how nature wants to heal us (read his blog post "A Mother's Nature" on flourishnourishinpantelleria.blogspot.com).

After selling a small but lucrative fresh-fish shop on Long Island, Lambert took over the family kitchen of Robert Wood "Woody" Johnson IV. Among his challenges was to help Johnson's daughter manage her juvenile-onset diabetes. "Woody himself," Lambert says, "is very proactive about staying healthy. I personally never saw him take a pharmaceutical." Not only did Lambert ensure his food helped manage Johnson's daughter's disease; he wanted her spirit to thrive as well. "As a little girl, she would come home crying from birthday parties because she couldn't eat the birthday cake," Lambert recalls. "So whenever she went to a birthday party, we offered to bring the cake. The children had no idea the cake was formulated for a diabetic, and a little girl felt included."

Over more than two decades serving the Johnson family and other elite clients, including actor Robert deNiro and Wall Street investment banker G. C. Anderson, word of Lambert's "healing with food" spread. "As you can imagine, the clients I worked for had a circle of friends and acquaintances with the resources to find and get the best treatments for their ailments. A lot of them started coming to me for advice and help," Lambert says. A voracious researcher, Lambert has identified and facilitated healing protocols based entirely on food for children and adults with C. diff, colitis, irritable bowel syndrome (IBS), food allergies, pre- and postnatal nutrition, Alzheimer's, juvenile and adult-onset diabetes, autism-spectrum disorder and lupus.

Regina W. of New York City approached Lambert in 2008 for help treating a C. diff infection contracted during a trip to Africa: "…My doctors wanted to give me more antibiotics, but instinctively I felt this was not the right approach, as my body has never liked antibiotics. Peter's protocol made sense; he explained how it worked to support and nourish the body and bring the *C. diff* back in to balance. It proved to be exactly the right approach for me…after several years of being so ill I could not work, I am now attending graduate school and will be looking for a job in the next few months. A recent stool test showed no signs of *C. diff.* Interestingly, *C. diff* is also not 'on my mind' anymore. The fear of it has left me, replaced by a better understanding of how to live in co-existence with the microbes inside me (and all of us)."

Josh Wagner, a New York City chiropractor, sought Lambert's help last year treating a stubborn rash: "After both an intern and internist took turns looking at it and suggesting rather elementary protocols (topical creams), it slightly faded, went away for a week, then returned immediately once I stopped using the cream. To me, it didn't make much sense that it was a dermatologic condition after reviewing the symptoms. I then enlisted help from Peter, because I know of his hunger for knowledge and research, particularly in the natural-healing realms, especially through food. At this time I also noticed a swollen lymph gland in my leg, which also concerned me. Peter provided an extraordinary amount of research and information for me to digest and get an understanding of what most likely was occurring…He gave me detailed steps to take to give my body the best chance to fight this off naturally, from the inside. After following his protocols, the rashes have disappeared in about a week, and I am confident they are not coming back."

"If anything," says Lambert, "what I offer to people who find me and request help is that I take the time to piece together the information they need to move forward. I never tell them that their doctors are wrong…I tell them how we are going to take responsibility for their life and realize the system they are relying on is overtaxed and not designed to find solutions to individual needs." And people continue to find Lambert on his tiny island; he laughs that his wife Amy snapped a photo of him standing up to his calves in the Mediterranean surf, a cell phone clamped to each ear, counseling clients.

"Peter has a serious hunger for knowledge," says Kim Hyttel, a Danish music producer and author who sought Lambert's counsel. "He just kept on investigating a subject until it made sense to him. That is passion for truth…I have seen him taking the micro-world of Pantelleria apart to understand its ecological system. His roots in food processing give him ample opportunities to discover the dangerous development of a medical/food processing conglomerate that wants to cure the health problems that stem from its own bad industrialized food with its own medical treatment. It's a self-contained business and a lethal one as well...honesty is a simple word, but a hard bargain. Peter is as honest as one can get."

"What I want people to understand," says Lambert, "is that if I have any 'motto,'...it's that 'choice is a function of awareness.' It applies to so many aspects of our lives, in terms of the industrialization of our basic needs, goods, services, and rights. We're told that 'big industry' makes things affordable; but the reality is that this is a subsidized affordability, which eventually implodes." Consistently with his many clients, Lambert says he hears two refrains: "'I had no choice,' or 'I was not aware.' It's such a demoralized way to be made to feel...I believe we're all here to be of service, and to empower each other to be the best of what we're meant to be."

Lofty ideals, for sure. So what's the currency of trade for such intense one-on-one consulting? Apparently, the kind of riches that don't come with decimal points. Lambert won't call it charity, but rather the priceless opportunity to restore dignity and "wholeness" to another human being. "The Hindu system of traditional medicine called Aryurveda," he adds, "insists that a practitioner must wear their money purse outside of their robes, so all could see how well they practiced. You see, Aryurvedic practitioners only get paid when they are well; they're not paid when the client is sick or not healthy. Now *that* is a system we all could embrace..."

Can Lambert produce hard data that proves his protocols work? Not to the standards of medical science, which would require clinical trials and randomized studies. It's unlikely any entity that could afford to run trials would do so, absent financial incentive. Nor, for the record, is Lambert unique in his passion for healing with food (when I Googled "healing with food" I got 145 million results). But Lambert's story at least lays out the notion that a compelling body of knowledge lies outside of traditional, "evidence-based medicine." It's worth investigating.

Maintaining Control—Through a Lifetime

Interior designer and Harvard instructor Cynthia Leibrock has rightly been called the "guru" of universal design—an approach where buildings, products and environments are inherently accessible to "both people without disabilities and people with disabilities." Leibrock defines it simply as "design for all people." Details like wide doorways, easy-to-reach amenities, and disappearing grab bars allow us to stay in our homes as long as possible without turning the home into a hospital.

With design projects that include the Betty Ford Center, the UCLA Medical Center, and a universal design exhibit at the Smithsonian under her belt, award-winning books to her name, and clients like Proctor and Gamble and Toyota inviting her to speak, why would I call someone like Leibrock a "health care hacker"? Because she too is challenging conformity, thinking "outside the box," and showing us a different way.

Like designer Michael Graves, Leibrock has worked to create universal design that's as beautiful as it is accessible. She's engineered it into her hospital designs—most recently, for instance, into a hospital project that specified antimicrobial carpet for slip-resistance, hard surfaces that kill germs on contact, and tables with pedestal bases instead of legs to accommodate those in wheelchairs. "Unfortunately," says Leibrock, "many of the details I put in got cut. They have to cut costs somewhere—and without consumers demanding it, these are the first items that get value-engineered out."

An AARP survey says 72 percent of people over age forty-five want to age in place, avoiding a nursing home and staying in their own home as long as possible. Yet in hospitals, nursing homes, and in-home health care, in both new construction and renovations, most projects still fail to incorporate many elements that would better serve aging populations, add to quality of life, and reduce the cost of care. In Leibrock's case, the conformity she's fighting is the public mindset. Aging boomers, the population most expected to drive demand, don't ask their contractors for universal design, perhaps not thinking they'll ever need it or shunning what they think is institutional-looking. "If you label a product as for the disabled or elderly," Leibrock says, "it's the kiss of death." So she emphasizes terms like great design, good health, and choice. (Her website is the gentle-sounding www. agingbeautifully.org.)

To show the world, and all the skeptical boomers in it, how beautiful and achievable universal design can be, Leibrock built a home to showcase the possibilities—and now lives in it. Perched atop a mountain an hour-and-a-half north of Denver, its striking glass-and-steel profile beckons like a work of art. Green Mountain Ranch is intended to be a showcase, laboratory, and training center for those interested in universal design. For six years, she and her husband lived with contractors as they installed nearly two hundred elements of universal design, some expensive, but half costing under fifty dollars. From her website:

"The project is proactive, using design elements to prevent injuries and to encourage a lifestyle that leads to health and longevity. The house is visitable by wheelchairs users, and adaptable to tall and short users, to people with low vision and low hearing, to those who want to do rehabilitation at home, and to those requiring a caregiver. All features are visually integrated, not advertising age or disability."

Most of the features can be seen in the fifty-plus photographs posted on her website, agingbeautifully.org/ranch. Many of the home's features go beyond accessibility to supporting a healthy lifestyle: A steam shower helps when cold or flu strikes. A magnetic induction wok and induction stove won't burn skin or set clothing on fire. A steam oven seals in nutrients. The exercise room is in the most beautiful part of the house, to encourage its use.

"You won't notice the grab bars, the gurney-accessible bathroom, the ceiling-track lift, or the accessible route through the house. It's there, but it's invisible. And," she says, "we suddenly needed all of it."

Soon after the home's renovation was complete, Leibrock's husband tore his Achilles tendon. This was right around the same time an old tennis injury required Leibrock herself to have a hip replacement. He was on a scooter, and she was using a walker. "The hospital was recommending a rehab facility," she says. "In other words, we were heading for *the home*. Instead we headed for *our* home, a safe and comfortable place with a seat in the steam shower, recessed wool area rugs, and beautiful wood floors which are slip-resistant, both wet and dry. After surgery we transferred from our car, wheeled into the accessible entry, pushed a button on the automatic door, and entered a space filled with healing natural light, beautiful views, soothing music, and so much more. This is a home for regeneration, our home for life." After a few months recuperating at home, the couple was ready for an Alaskan vacation that included kayaking, biking, hiking, and canoeing.

Listening to Leibrock, I couldn't help but think of my own father, who'd worked so hard to leave the hospital and rehab center and go home again. But by the time he was finally discharged, he was too weak to manage the stairs in the split-level home where my parents had raised four children. Instead he'd spent his last weeks in a condo he'd barely seen before. Over the years, after my mother's knee replacement and at other times, we'd offered to help our parents install a full bathroom downstairs. But they'd always insisted, "We're fine." Everyone wants to cross that bridge when they come to it.

That bridge had come and gone. My father would never again enter his home of forty-two years.

Ultimately we'd had two weeks to find a place my father and mother liked well enough and to move them in. A realtor had taken us on a hastily arranged tour of accessible condos. My father, sprung from the hospital for a few hours, had led an entourage that included me, my mother, the realtor, a nurse, and a physical therapist. They'd wheeled him from unit to unit, weighing this layout versus that one, the relative appeal of paint and carpet colors, an eat-in kitchen versus a dining room. I remember a surreal whirlwind, on some levels almost comic in its brisk intensity. But underneath there'd been a recognition of how different life would be. There would be no more tomato garden for Dad; none of the units even had a balcony or patio. My mother's precious peonies, such a joy to her when they bloomed each spring, would be cut and treasured by strangers.

We'd been lucky that between us siblings we managed to finance and secure the condo prior to the house being sold. But in the frantic pace of moving everything so quickly, many things had been lost. My father's prized coin and stamp collections, dating back to his childhood. His father's wristwatch. For other things, there had simply been no room. Not that these things were precious to anyone but my parents. But still, they'd been a loss, on top of so many other losses.

So when Leibrock told me about her easy transition into a home she'd designed for just such an eventuality, I was overwhelmed with a feeling of how different it might have been for my father. But instead, I remembered how diminished his spirit became in the last weeks of his life, as he lost control over his choices. I also wished I'd been more insistent with my parents before the opportunity had slipped away from us.

What Leibrock is really selling is not just design or accessibility—it's control. Or as she says in her website, "returning authority to the patient."

Where does Leibrock's singular mission come from? "My younger brother has schizophrenia. When I was younger, he was in institutions and nursing homes where the environment had a horrible impact on him. But when he went to a halfway house, I saw what a difference a supportive environment could make." Years later, Leibrock became involved with a Bible study group that helped focus her real vision: to create environments that are supportive for older and disabled people.

"I want people to know that no matter whether they have mental or physical challenges, they are only disabled if they can't do what they want to do. Architecture can eliminate disability by design. If you are in a house where you can do what you want to do, you're not disabled anymore."

Leibrock's latest book, *Design Details for Health*, offers an eye-opening glimpse at how other countries have entirely different models of housing for people of different abilities. Read about how dementia patients in Sweden become much more high functioning by living in well-designed group homes. Or how the elderly in the Netherlands move into an "apartment for life." They will never have to move to assisted living or skilled nursing. These apartment complexes integrate both the community support and the medical care they may need. Both the Swedish and Dutch models are extremely cost effective. What frustrates Leibrock is that the United States "is stuck with archaic building codes, as well as Medicare and Medicaid policies in desperate need of revisions".

Here, too, change isn't likely to come without pressure from the public. "The biggest challenge of my career is to create consumer demand," she says.

For those who want to be more proactive than my parents were (and I hope you do), Leibrock's book contains a wealth of tips to prepare your home so you can "age beautifully" and in place. She was kind enough to let me excerpt the list and provide sources and insider tips for you and your contractor. Find the list in the Resources section in the back of this book.

Dignity—in Retail

To designer and architect Michael Graves, paralyzed from a rare virus since 1993, the ultimate indignity came one day while he was a patient in a top-ranked hospital: "I was in a Hoyer lift." (a body sling mounted to a metal structure, used to help lift and move a patient). "The nurse was moving me from the bed to the chair, when another nurse came to the door and called to her friend, 'Come on, it's time for our break.' After initially saying that she had to finish moving me first, my nurse changed her mind…and went on break with her colleague. So she left me dangling in the sling, midway between the bed and chair."

"What did you do?" I asked, horrified.

"My room was close enough to the nurses' station that I was able to call out and eventually get somebody to come and help me."

Graves tells this story to illustrate how important it is for a hospital to have a culture of care—and how egregious harm to body and spirit can occur when it's absent. "These workers aren't bad people. I don't blame them. They may have been trained medically, but they haven't been trained in any culture of care." Graves points to how other companies work from the top down to create this unified approach. "Apple, for instance, has its VP of sales interview and train managers, who in turn train secondary managers, who in turn interview and train every single worker and helper, so the interaction with the customer is consistently up to the same high standard. That's what it takes." Absent this level of attention, Graves says, Apple might lose a customer's business. In a hospital, the loss can be much worse.

Graves' better designs for hospital furniture, shower chairs, and canes that zip into satchels offer a glimpse into a future where every person's dignity and control is honored as a birthright, regardless of physical limitation. However, Graves' crusade to put such tools in others' hands is tempered by realism. While Stryker has partnered with his firm to bring many of these products to market, for the most part you'll have to go through a distributor and order them online. Like crutches, walkers, and other mobility tools, if you can find them at retail stores at all, it will most likely be in a separate durable medical equipment (DME) store. (A notable exception is pharmacy chain CVS, which operates twenty-eight CVS "Home Health" locations around the country.)

The obvious question: what about Target stores, where Graves-design products became iconic of "good design accessible to all"? After fifteen years designing for Target, Graves' relationship with the giant retailer came to an end in early 2012. "I tried like crazy to get them to sell the new mobility designs," he told me. "They said they'd do it when Walmart does it. And Walmart's not gonna do it until customers ask for it."

Graves hopes for help from a group of customers "that's the right demographic and the right age: 'sandwich moms'." These are moms assisting aging parents while raising their own families. According to Consumerist. com research conducted in 2009, "There's a huge unmet need for products and services that help care for aging parents now and in the future. While there are myriad offerings to help consumers plan for their own retirement and the care and education of their children, there are relatively few resources to prepare for the inevitable responsibility of caring for the aging population. Brands—even those not associated with serving the aged—can do much, much more to capitalize on the support and comfort they already provide, and to provide it in new ways."

Many of these sandwich moms, says Graves, "would pay a few more dollars for better choices, but they don't even know there *are* better choices." If we figure out how to make her aware, "it's her voice that'll make noise… *that* will change things."

Another new dynamic entering the landscape: soldiers returning from combat in Iraq and Afghanistan. With advances in treating grievous injuries, many more troops are coming home alive—and facing new challenges. "Some twenty thousand of these kids are paralyzed from the waist or chest down," says Graves. "They're not only trying to rebuild their lives, but a lot of them can't find jobs. Many of them are re-upping in the service." Graves' firm was commissioned to help design model homes to accommodate these vets; the Wounded Warrior Homes, at the Army's Fort

Belvoir in Virginia, served as prototypes for nineteen similar homes now under construction. The intention is to create "living laboratories" where occupants can test and give feedback on new features. As with Leibrock's showcase home in Colorado, "you walk into the home and have no idea it's specifically designed for mobility issues. Everything is integrated and elegant," says Graves.

Is it possible these wounded warriors might extend their heroism beyond the theater of battle by inspiring a more mainstream awareness of the need for universal design? "All of us will need some adaptations in our lifetime," says Graves. "Our hope is this work for wounded warriors will spark further movement within the Department of Defense, and that the trend will carry over to elderly housing, and housing for all of us."

Meantime Graves looks hopefully toward the future. In the pipeline for his firm's health care product designs is a transport wheelchair for hospitals the firm is developing with Stryker. "It will dramatically improve patients' experience being moved around hospitals," says Ben Wintner, Director of Business Development for Michael Graves & Associates. "We're very focused on creating a comprehensive collection of products for the home that make it possible for people to age in place independently and safely." It's quite a laundry list of products, including those for "...mobility, bath safety, aids for daily living, medication management, furniture, and architectural products like windows, bath fixtures, kitchen fixtures, and ramps. We think there is going to be a huge market for these products, and people are going to demand high-quality, well-designed home health care products. We are actively pursuing manufacturing and distribution partners to make this a reality."

But even as Graves realizes his vision of an expanded new generation of empowering tools, the smallest things—literally, the smallest— remain some of the most vexing. I learned this myself recently while accompanying my lifelong friend, Katie, whose son got married recently, to the hotel where her twenty-three-year-old daughter Molly would be staying. Molly has cerebral palsy and has been in a wheelchair all her life. Concerned especially that the shower be accessible, Katie and I asked to tour the exact room where Molly and her aide would be staying. As promised, the spaces and doorways in the room were wide, and the sink was open underneath to accommodate her wheelchair. However Katie took one look at the "roll-in shower," and her face fell. "That threshold," she said, pointing to the half-inch-high slab of stone at the entrance of the shower, "will stop her cold."

Katie knows the hotel is well meaning, and so is the contractor who probably added the threshold to make it "look nice." But to a person in a rolling shower chair, whose combined weight is a couple of hundred pounds, that "little bump" works like wheel chocks on an airplane.

I brought this up to Graves and his team. "You travel all over the world," I said. "Is this a situation you find a lot?" What I didn't expect was for the group to erupt in laughter. "You have no idea," said Graves. "You've really hit a sore spot. It drives me nuts." Like Leibrock, Grave's solution is a "trench" drain that replaces the threshold, is flush with the floor, and works beautifully. "There's no reason to do anything else," he says.

It seems to come down to consciousness—something Graves promotes by having new hires at his firm spend time in a wheelchair. As for the world at large, Graves' story about how he was left dangling in midair in a Hoya lift, as wrong as it was on every level, is also indicative of the far more insidious harm that occurs when we devalue a person's basic human dignity—or shrug when it happens. Bring up the subject of indignities suffered by patients, and see what stories come up—like a grown woman sobbing for a tissue at 3 a.m. because the bed table with the tissue box has been moved out of reach (and no one's answering the call button), or a grandmother, asking to be taken to the bathroom, being told, "It's shift change. If you can't wait, you're going to have to go in the bed." These humiliations, both large and small, degrade not just the person experiencing them; they diminish all of us.

A final word on health care hackers—these outliers with a singular vision of how to take various system components widely accepted by the masses and do a "one-better": I applaud your cobbling together something new, imaginative, and visionary, as well as the heart that drives you to keep going long past the need for validation or accolades. As Margaret Mead said, "Never doubt that a small group of committed people can change the world; indeed, it's the only thing that ever has."

Critical Opportunities for Healthcare

Look to other industries for inspiration and solutions.

Critical Opportunities for Patients & Families

Investigate "hacker solutions". Learnings and truth can come from many sources. Seek solutions and alternatives that fit into the way you want to live.

9 If IKEA designed health care...

it would live to innovate

In IKEA's business philosophy, the whole matter should be inscribed as a golden rule: regard every problem as a possibility.
—Ingvar Kamprad and Bertil Torekull,
Leading by Design: The IKEA Story

Innovation is part of IKEA's DNA. Remember in chapter 5 we said that its "flat-pack" concept began with an employee taking the legs off a table so it would fit in the trunk of a car? That's only part of the story. Fact is, IKEA was already assembling its own furniture by then (which is why the on-the-spot disassembly was even possible in the first place). Competitors had pressured suppliers to boycott IKEA, trying to force the low-cost retailer out of business. Instead, the boycott spurred IKEA to take over ownership of the entire design and manufacturing process. While turning a "problem into a possibility," IKEA also discovered one of its most iconic and successful innovations: flat-pack furniture (also making delivery unnecessary, since customers could take the stuff home). Many other innovations followed, like putting restaurants in the middle of its stores and offering playrooms for kids. Where do their ideas come from?

"There is absolutely an expectation at IKEA that, with our flat organization structure, everyone contributes," says IKEA's US marketing chief, Bill Agee. "Whoever you are within the IKEA organization, you're expected to contribute your ideas—your new ideas, your old ideas, or whatever it may be—and every idea is welcome. That means that many more innovative ideas rise to the surface, get watched, and actually get executed than in a traditional, hierarchical organization."[138]

Its latest innovative idea launches IKEA into a brave new world: consumer electronics. In April 2012 the company unveiled the Uppleva, an all-in-one entertainment center that merges consumer electronics with the furniture that has traditionally housed them. It's an HDTV, Blu-Ray player, and 2.1 surround-sound stereo packed seamlessly into a single, visually customizable unit. IKEA's early marketing says that it eliminates unsightly wires and multiple remote controls, something customers the world over want, according to IKEA. The Uppleva will be available in the US in 2013.

Innovation—reworking the system we have now—is critical in health care. It's the only way an increasing number of people are going to get quality care at a cost that the nation can afford.

Easier said than done, of course, for all the reasons we've looked at so far: it's a highly fragmented industry, with a hierarchical culture resistant to change and a payment system that rewards providers for quantity rather than quality of care. It's been slow to adopt technologies like electronic medical records that have the potential to make care more efficient and safer for patients. And as we've seen with Peter Pronovost and his checklist campaign, even when simple new practices have been shown to improve care and reduce error, hospitals and doctors have been slow to adopt them.

Some hospitals are doing something very IKEA-like: asking staff for ideas. Penn Medicine in Philadelphia put out the call for "Your Big Idea"—and staff delivered. More than 1,750 ideas were submitted from 1,400 participants. Ideas ranged from installing digital mapping and signage so patients wouldn't lose their way, to setting up an "almost home" room where patients awaiting discharge could sit in reclining chairs and use the Internet, freeing up much-needed hospital beds.

The government is determined to be part of the "ideas" solution. The new health care law also created a Center for Medicare and Medicaid Innovation. It's paying out one billion dollars in grants as part of its mission to identify, test, and spread new ways of delivering and paying for care. But, as then-CMS director Don Berwick warned, "None of this will be easy. Government cannot and should not do this alone."

Nor does it have to. Health care futurist Joe Flower says the private sector already sees the giant prize at the center of the labyrinth of changing health care: "We could do it better, for less. And more and more companies are heading straight for that prize."[139]

Flower points to retail clinics like CVS/Caremark, which in the last fifteen years has swallowed up half a dozen other drugstore chains, growing from 1,400 stores to over 7,000. In 2006, it bought MinuteClinic, a chain of retail clinics, and began expanding it to almost 600 locations in 25 states. It's using this massive market footprint to do something about chronic disease, starting with diabetes. It aggressively gets out and works with patients by, for instance, sending a nurse to your house to show you how to test your glucose level, how to use insulin, and how to regulate your diet to keep the disease in check.

GE Healthcare, with 46,000 employees, headquartered in the UK, is also using its considerable influence to improve health care. One of the largest vendors of medical equipment in the world, and highly focused on quality, it's set out on a major program involving all its major executives, down to the manager level, to better understand the customer. That includes how the industry works, how it makes its money, how it gets things done, and why quality and efficiency in processes are only beginning to be understood across much of health care. They are doing this, GE executives tell Flower, "not only to work with their customers better, but also partly to influence their customers, to educate them about the way GE thinks about quality and efficiency. As a GE executive told Flower, "We see that health care simply has to change, and it will change, to be more lean and efficient. If we help lead that charge, we will be identified in the customers' minds with a whole new way of working more efficiently, with less variation, and better quality."

Technology tools are also putting innovation in the palm of the hand. The smart phone and smart tablet are revolutionizing how we do everyday things, and they've barely begun to make their mark in health care. In his book *The Creative Destruction of Medicine,* cardiologist Eric Topol lays out his vision for how people will be using new technologies to start running common medical tests, skipping office visits, and sharing their data with people other than their physicians. An example: "I have this device where I can measure my glucose every minute and download it to my phone—you attach a sensor with a little needle and you wear it on your stomach, or under your arm. Seeing your glucose every minute on your phone, it really changes your lifestyle. You ask yourself, "Do I really need that piece of cake? No, because I don't want to stress out my pancreas."[140]

Topol recently used a prototype of another device attached to his iPhone to diagnose a heart attack in a passenger aboard a flight at 35,000 feet. The device uses two built-in sensors connected to an app. "You put your fingers on the sensors, or put them up to your chest, and it works like an ECG [echocardiogram] that you read in real time on your phone."

The smart phone and the smart tablet stand to put real control in patients' hands, too. As Flower says: "The core of it is not the device, it is the combination of cheap or free apps on a relatively open platform for which anyone can design."

Some facilities are harnessing technology to improve the patient's understanding and experience of care. The Mayo Clinic has begun using content- and app-loaded iPads to help guide patients through their hospital experience (it's also posted a video depicting iPad use on its YouTube page). Each heart-surgery patient is given an iPad to help them visualize and prepare for their plan of care. The app is tailored to the patient's daily schedule, patient education information, and notes about planning for recovery.

Another iPad app customizes the MRI experience, which is often intimidating and scary (your whole body is inserted into a sarcophagus-like tube, sometimes for hours, to the sound of loud banging noises). The app lets patients select lighting, music, images, and video to be available during their scan. The images are embedded via LED lights in the walls and ceilings of the suite, and controlled by the iPad. Patients can also dock their own iPhones or iPods to listen to their own music or watch their own videos.

An iPad app called OnPatient allows hospitals to check patients in via iPad instead of paper forms and clipboards. Health care providers can create a customized check-in form. Then when patients fill out the form for the first time, they input their personal, demographic, and insurance information, take a profile photo, review their medications and allergies, and their records are saved for future use.

A cost-effective and truly rewarding use of these tablets is for virtual physician-patient communication. By simply using the iPad's Facetime feature, physicians and patients can video chat about the patient's recovery progress. Henry Ford Hospital has been using this feature, which also comes on the newer iPhone and the latest generation iPod touch, to conduct a new initiative called "telerounding." Not only does this practice help physicians on the clinical side, it gives patients the positive feeling of personalized care even when they are miles away from the hospital. (Of course many physicians are already using iPad apps one on one, as a teaching tool to educate and inform patients about their medical conditions.)

Topol and Flower believe that consumers teaming up with innovators in the medical-digital world are a key to forcing change. But they acknowledge such changes can pose a huge threat to the revenue streams providers have come to rely on.

Consider a device called the Vscan, manufactured by General Electric. It's a portable device about the size of book, with a wand connected by a wire. Says Topol: "I haven't used a stethoscope as a cardiologist in about two years now. As part of a routine physical exam, I do a full echo of a patient's heart. I see the valves, the chamber, the whole thing. Why would I listen to the heart go lub dub?…And each echo exam is free once you buy the thing, which is about $7,000. It costs something like $800 every time you send someone to the echo lab, and they do this ritualistic 45-minute study. I do this as part of the physical exam in one to two minutes."

Why isn't it used by all cardiologists today? "Because they don't get reimbursed," says Topol. "The hospital loses a charge of greater than $500 and the doctor loses his fee. There are 20 million echocardiograms done a year. How many billions of dollars is that?"

That same issue underlies that fact that most of us patients can't communicate with our physicians via e-mail. Unlike a lawyer, who bills every time he hits the "reply" button, physicians are not paid for their time. They are paid by the "widget." The patient visit is the doctor's version of the widget. "Anything physicians do to prepare for that visit, communicate between visits, review the tests induced by that visit, or consult about your problem with another physician is gratis."[141] Cigna and Aetna have piloted programs that pay doctors for making "virtual house calls" through e-mail.

Electronic Medical Records are creating new efficiencies and eliminating mistakes and redundancies, which is why the federal government is pouring billions of dollars into health care IT. (A February 2011 survey of 600 physicians by *Consumer Reports* found that 37 percent of physicians now keep patient records entirely electronically—up from 24 percent in its 2007 survey.) Successful systems, like the VA Hospitals', have improved accountability, integrated services, and improved patient safety.

But integrating IT can be a painful operation. Why?

1. **The user interface "stinks,"** says health care IT futurist Jeff Goldsmith.[142] "Crucial information about a patient's current condition is either entombed deep in the record, 12 clicks below the main screen, or somehow hasn't reached the record yet." "Looking for relevant information in an electronic medical record is like reading *Where's Waldo,*" says one physician, as reported in JAMA.[143] "Ironically, this physician "...started to handwrite a list of new developments on index cards so that he can refer to them at the bedside."

2. **"Patient who"?** "The new computer system also drew my attention from the patient," says physician Alexander Friedman, MD, in a blog post. "I often stood turned away, typing on the computer mounted against the wall, occasionally turning my head over my shoulder to make eye contact...our patients deserve better."

3. **It's led to more testing.** A study published in the March 2012 *Health Affairs* found "office-based physicians who have access to

electronic records of patient care are actually more likely to order additional imaging tests and laboratory tests than doctors who rely on paper records."

Says Pronovost of Hopkins: "Ironically, healthcare has invested significantly in technology, but it's the only industry for which technology hasn't helped productivity or safety...[I]n part, that's because we've invested in individual devices, but we haven't looked at integrating them as systems."[143]

In addition, the computers themselves can be frustrating. Writes Rosemary Gibson in The Battle Over Healthcare:

...computer failures are frequent occurrences, not rare events. Systems often "time out" quickly and require password reentry. Screens freeze and the systems must be rebooted and previous work that was lost needs to be redone. Each malfunction requires troubleshooting the source of the problem, which takes time away from patient care. The computer becomes the patient.

Mobile computers offer special challenges. Because they rely on wireless systems, they may lose connectivity in some locations in the hospital. Because computers are used almost continuously, there is limited time to recharge their batteries...Nurses have a name for the mobile computers on wheels: "COWs." The wheels can stick—like the wheels on a grocery cart that will not turn. Nurses have to drag the computers and their carts, which weigh more than sixty pounds. The computers are in constant use, and protocols to maintain them are not well established...None of these operational pitfalls suggests that electronic medical records should not be used. The health care industry has been an unabashed laggard in adoption of electronic information systems. They are not an immediate panacea, though, and the unintended safety consequences are real in the mad dash to use them."[146]

Squarely in the cross-hairs during this "sausage-making" process is *the patient.*

Asking the Patient: What do YOU Want?

Doctors who ask this question are transforming patients' lives for the better, leading to fewer hospitalizations, fewer ER visits, fewer missed work days, and above all else, a heightened sense of well-being with better health and a lower use of the health system. This improvement is even more dramatic when nurses and trained counselors regularly follow up with questions like: Is your condition inhibiting your life? Does your disease make it hard to cope from day to day?

Maureen Bisognano, President and CEO of the Institute for Healthcare Improvement, offers this suggestion: "A whiteboard next to every patient bed. On that whiteboard, write daily (and longer-term) goals with the patient. Develop these goals during multidisciplinary rounds with the care team and the patient or family member.

"The whiteboards should include clinical goals, like lowering BP [blood pressure], and patient-directed goals like the one I heard from my colleague in Saskatchewan, Dr. Susan Shaw. Her patient's daughter excitedly greeted her one day, showing her a piece of paper on which the mother had written, 'My goals: 1) heal this broken body; 2) cut grass.' The patient simply wanted to be healthy enough to mow her lawn. Dr. Shaw noted the inspirational power this wish had on her and her team, and the clear direction it gave them about how to plan the patient's care."[147]

"The logic is simple," writes columnist Laura Landro of the *Wall Street Journal*. "People are more likely to manage their condition properly when they have more accessible, personal goals, like being able to do more at work or keep up with their kids, instead of focusing only on comparatively abstract targets like blood-sugar levels. And that, in turn, leads to much better health. Numerous studies show that when people have a higher sense of well-being, they have fewer hospitalizations and emergency-room visits, miss fewer days of work, and use less medication. They're also more productive at work and more engaged in the community."[148]

The magic of this simple approach is in respecting patients enough to let us make our own (informed) choices. Some who've worked for years in traditional medicine and behavioral health see this as the *only* way to truly impact behavior and change health outcomes. For example, the husband and wife team of Bill and Katharine White spent decades as top administrators in traditional medicine and behavioral health. In 2012 they launched AdvoGeneX (AdvoGeneX.com), a "comprehensive wellness platform" that taps into a client's personal motivations and barriers to adopting healthier behaviors and "activates" them to change.[149]

"We assumed one of our senior clients wanted to beat his cancer so he could spend additional years with his grandchildren", said co-founder Bill White. "What we learned though through 'coaching and activation', is that what he really wanted was to find love again. This formed an entirely new agenda for his wellness activation plan, which continuously engaged and motivated him to be empowered and in charge. We collaboratively developed the plan, but he was the one that drove a truck through it. The change in his thinking and behavior was amazing…as were his clinical test results, to the point where his Dana-Farber team of physicians refer to it as unexplainable."

"If we truly want to prolong quality living and save lives—it has to be all about helping and educating clients and patients, and much less about fixing hospitals and providers," adds Katharine White. "Changing to a patient- or client-centric healthcare culture will ultimately improve the performance of those individuals and institutions delivering care and treatment."[150]

Doctors did not invent the rules in the perverse and bloated system in which they must operate. But we need our physicians to believe something better is possible.

Peter Pronovost, the "checklist pioneer" doctor at Johns Hopkins, says improvement starts with a dream—a conception—that we can be better. In a blog post, he refers to the eye-rolling that greeted singer Susan Boyle when she first strolled on stage in *Britain's Got Talent* and announced she wanted to be singing star. Who was this frumpy and awkward middle-aged woman? "I suspect she had her own doubts," he writes. "Yet she had the courage to try. She believed in herself and stunned the audience with her voice…This same self-doubt exists in patient safety. I know because I had plenty of uncertainty about my ability to reduce patient harm. More than a decade ago, we decided to reduce central line-associated bloodstream infections on one intensive care unit…most of the physicians thought it couldn't be done. Sick people get infected, they said. These infections just happen. In our own way, we felt frumpy and awkward…We focused on consistently following those practices shown by evidence to reduce them…[but] as compliance rose, the rates went to nearly zero, and the doubts disappeared…"[151]

Like Pronovost, and Laura Esserman who pioneered the "everything under one roof" Breast Cancer Clinic at UCSF, Don Berwick had a vision of what "better" could look like. His success at "selling" his vision made medical history.

An Innovation Legend

In 2004, while Berwick was leading the Institute for Healthcare Improvement, IHI researchers had determined that 1 in 10 patients experienced a "defect" in their medical care (such as not getting needed antibiotics on time). Berwick knew this meant that thousands of patients were dying unnecessarily. His insight was that hospitals could take a page from the rigorous process improvement that benefited other industries, like the auto industry (specifically Toyota), which practiced rigid quality control.

Berwick's ideas were well-supported by research. But what could he do to force change on the industry? IHI had only 75 employees. But that didn't stop Berwick.

At IHI's annual convention in 2004, he laid down the gauntlet. "Here is what I think we should do," he said to a packed room of hospital administrators. "I think we should save 100,000 lives. And I think we should do that by June 14, 2006—18 months from today. Some is not a number; soon is not a time. Here's the number: 100,000. Here's the time: June 14, 2006—9 AM."

The crowd was astonished. But Berwick was quite serious. IHI proposed six specific interventions to make health care safer (such as raising the heads of patients on ventilators, which prevent bacteria from the stomach getting into the airways, known to reduce ventilator-associated pneumonia by 34 %).

But first, there was a big hurdle to clear. Hospitals weren't keen on admitting they were responsible for needless deaths. Berwick faced it head-on. Joining him on the stage was the mother of a young girl who'd been killed by medical error. Said Sorrel King: "I know that if this campaign had been in place four or five years ago that Josie would be fine". Another guest, the head of the North Carolina Hospital Association added, "it's time to do the right thing".

The effort was structured and rolled out like a political campaign. Within two months of Berwick's speech, over a thousand hospitals had signed on. (To do so, the hospital CEO simply signed a one-page pledge.) IHI "precinct captains" took it from there, providing research, instructions and training. As recounted in *Switch: How to Change Things When Change is Hard:* "The friction in the system was substantial. Adopting the IHI interventions required hospitals to overcome decades' worth of habits and routines ... but the adopting hospitals were seeing dramatic results, and their visible successes attracted more hospitals to join the campaign."[152]

Eighteen months later, at precisely 9 AM on June 14, 2006, Berwick again took the stage to announce the results: "Hospitals enrolled in the 100,000 Lives Campaign have collectively prevented an estimated 122,000 avoidable deaths and, as importantly, have begun to institutionalize new standards of care that will continue to save lives and improve health outcomes in the future." The crowd was euphoric. Berwick and his small team at IHI had gotten thousands of hospitals to change their behavior.

His vision had been laid out eloquently eighteen months before: "The names of the patients whose lives we save can never be known. Our contribution will be what did *not* happen to them. And, though they are unknown, we will know that mothers and fathers are at graduations and weddings they would have missed, and that grandchildren will know grandparents they might never have known, and holidays will be taken, and work completed, and books read, and symphonies heard, and gardens tended that, without our work, would never have been."[153]

"Conceptually," wrote Peter Pronovost and Bob Wachter in a subsequent analysis of the campaign, "the idea of a campaign catalyzed by front-line workers 'doing the right thing' was attractive. IHI, an organization with a large reservoir of established credibility, a highly respected and charismatic leader, and close connections to many hospitals and health care systems, was well positioned to lead such a campaign, despite (or perhaps because of) its absence of regulatory authority or formal role in the health care hierarchy." [154]

But, they added, it's not necessarily the numbers that made history: "…the actual mortality data were supplied without audit by the more than 3,000 participating hospitals, and 14% of the hospitals submitted no data at all … Nevertheless, in a crowded marketplace of accreditation standards, regulations, reporting, and cajoling, IHI succeeded in establishing and promoting a set of achievable goals for American hospitals. Perhaps this was the most noteworthy achievement of the campaign: the generation of unprecedented amounts of social pressure to participate."[154 155]

The Ultimate Change Agent: The Power of Many

Whether from a fall down the stairs, a car crash, disease, clogged arteries, or worn-out body parts, a trip to the hospital is an ever-present possibility. Who will be your best ally? Find yourself a primary care physician who listens, respects you, and embraces shared decision-making. "If your relationship with your physician is such that you fear 'being fired' for advocating for your own health, you have a problem," says Steve Wilkins, a former hospital executive who blogs about patient-physician communication at Mind The Gap. "[If] your physician does not respect you or your opinion…life's too short, and there are too many good physicians out there to waste your time on a bad one. But before you leave, tell the doctor why you are leaving, and that you will be sharing your experience with your 5,000 Twitter followers and 10,000 Facebook fans."

That kind of power, wielded by patients in an organized way, can ultimately change health care.

Some patient advocates are counting on it. Regina Holliday is one of them.

Regina is a Washington, DC-based artist, speaker and author. Her plunge into patient advocacy began when her husband Fred was diagnosed with kidney cancer in 2009. The ensuing weeks were brutal, with compassion by many providers sadly lacking, and made worse by the fact that though Fred had just secured his "dream job" teaching at a local college, the medical insurance had not yet kicked in. Regina, an art teacher, struggled to get her husband appropriate care during eleven weeks of continuous hospitalization at five different facilities. When Fred died eleven weeks after diagnosis, leaving her to raise their two little boys, Regina found her mission: to express her frustration, outrage and insights through art.

She began by painting a huge mural on the side of a building near her home in Washington, DC, depicting Fred Holliday at the center and the trial they'd experienced. The painting was entitled "73 cents"—the price Regina was told she'd have to pay per page for a copy of her husband's medical record, and after a wait of twenty-one days.

The mural got a great deal of national attention and encouraged Regina to continue painting. Her work is a visual reminder of the patient at the center (or too often, far from the center) of care, policy debate and/or technical applications. She's also an accomplished student of health information technology, or HIT. Her talent extends to her passion in her public speaking, and her blog posts at Reginaholliday.blogspot.com.

As of January 2013, Regina had spoken at 76 venues in two years, including keynotes for major medical organizations in Australia and South Korea. When she's not at the podium, she can frequently be found on the fringes of the room, easel perched on a paint-splotched drop cloth, creating a visual metaphor of what she's hearing and seeing. (Many of these paintings grace the lobbies and foyers of the organizations that contract her to speak). She also founded "The Walking Gallery of Health Care", painting personal "medical journeys" on the backs of business jackets, which are then worn by providers and patient advocates to medical conferences and events. The jackets both represent the patient's story, and prompt conversation and awareness. (The one she painted for me is called "Invasion of the *C.diff*") At this writing the gallery has 200 "Walkers" and counting, wearing 220 jackets. Regina painted 199 of them. (See photos at her blog).

I saw—or rather heard—Regina in action in May 2012. She and I were two of the dozen or so patient advocates invited to attend a webinar by the national Partnership for Patients (PfP), a national initiative to reduce medical harm and hospital re-admissions. Frustrated that relatively little time was built into the itinerary for patient advocate voices, Regina let the organizers know it. After the call, she turned immediately to social media. Within five minutes, she'd already secured the URL PartnershipWithPatients.

com—emphasis on the "with" (I found out after looking into getting it myself). Minutes later she launched a Facebook page with the same name. By evening, nearly 130 people had joined her Facebook group. Weeks later she'd secured sponsors and launched plans for the first ever Partnership With Patients Summit to be held in Kansas City, complete with travel scholarships so a good number of patient advocates could attend. (See Afterword in this book for an update on the Summit.) In doing what it takes to fix health care, Regina is fearless. "I will not stop," she says. "After what happened to Fred, there's nothing they can do to me."

While no one person, place or thing creates the "tipping point" in any social movement, history tells us an iconic event can ignite the public passion that fuels real change. It happened when the nation rallied behind Rosa Parks to spark the civil rights movement; when Ralph Nader's book *Unsafe at Any Speed* made dangerous automobiles safer, and when airline passengers stranded on the tarmac for hours, with no food and overflowing toilets, demanded and won a Congressional "Passenger's Bill of Rights".

What will health care consumers' watershed event be? A famous person taking up the cause, like Katie Couric urging us to get colon cancer screening after losing her husband to the disease? A buzz-generating book or movie that dominates book clubs, morning talk shows, and water cooler conversations, the way the movie *Philadelphia* changed our thinking and public policy about AIDS? The work of one or more of the patient advocates you've met on these pages?

Or will reform arise from the nascent "Occupy Healthcare" (OH) movement (www.occupyhealthcare.net)? This newest member of the "Occupy" family can be found at a virtual "street corner" rather than in tents at Zuccotti Park. But it appears to have tapped a similar, burgeoning passion for change. It's the brainchild of Dr. Benjamin Miller, a psychologist at the University of Colorado School of Medicine who speaks nationally about health policy (though he quickly defers ownership of the Occupy Healthcare movement to the "team" he's creating). Miller launched the OH website in late 2011 as "a way for the community to come together and discuss how we can demand more from health care." In just a few months, the site has grown pretty quickly via online efforts like Google Groups, Facebook, and Twitter.

This is not about me. It is not about you. This is about us.

—OccupyHealthcare.net website

Miller, like Advo-Caring.com's Bill and Katharine White, believes modern medicine fails when it insists on treating physical health as separate from mental health. "Our decisions in health care are often driven by those with a limited world view…policy makers, administrators, and bureaucrats who care about the wrong things," he says. Unlike Occupy Wall Street, OH promotes clear principles, wishing to change patient, provider, payer, and legislative attitudes around health care. Early contributors to the website's blog, including several practicing physicians, seem credentialed and committed. "One of the differences in our movement," says Miller, "is that we're driven by a multidisciplinary group of providers, patients, and policy makers, committed to our life goal: to change health care. We have the reach and respect in the community to do it. We know the issues well enough to write about them in a way that the community can understand, and hopefully do something with," he says.

Miller describes the need to bring together the "disconnected brilliance" that already exists around the country. "I think communities have answers… programs that work. The state of Maine, for instance, created a program that integrated a mental-health component into health care, and discovered it not only led to better outcomes, but it cost less. We need to build out these successes regionally, then nationally."

Why doesn't policy change happen more quickly or more often? Miller says it's a combination of no business case (the primary driver of most policy decisions), no common language among all the players, and no compelling voice to lead the charge. Echoing the concern of universal design maven Cynthia Leibrock, he says patients and families also don't seem to want to be part of the revolution—at least not yet. "We need to figure out what kinds of things, what options, would get them to do things differently."

Ultimately, Miller says, two things drive policy change: money and stories. As we've seen in these pages, the way we pay for health care is shifting. Whether the change is incremental or seismic, and whether the patient benefits in the end, depends on how strong the pressure is and where it comes from. As for stories, he invites everyone to visit the "virtual street corner" at occupyhealthcare.net to share them. (Click "Our Commitment" on the website to see who's taken the pledge, bearing a sign that reads: "I am ready to build the health care system America deserves." When you do, imagine thousands or millions of these images, compressed into a digital collage, sort of a "virtual AIDS quilt".)

For now, Miller has no plans to incorporate Occupy Healthcare, or to fundraise. It's partly due to limited bandwidth: "For a lot of us who've signed on, this is our second professional home." There's also no talk of setting up committees or campaigns or agendas. "What we want to do is to bring together the dream team...and to collect voices, stories, and momentum," Miller says. "The only ownership we have is leadership...to bring a voice to the voiceless."

What will become of this noble venture? Could the Occupy Healthcare movement, stepping thoughtfully in the wake of its more strident and less-focused older cousin, help create the "tipping point" so needed in health care?

Why wait to find out? Patients, in large and small ways, can be change agents. Visit a health care blog and leave a comment, or post something interesting or helpful on your Facebook page. Tweet a message about the great (or poor) care you got at the clinic or hospital. Do some homework before you visit the doctor. Ask thoughtful questions. Thank him or her for taking extra minutes with you. Share your story (or post your photo) at occupyhealthcare.net. Visit some of the websites you're read about. Ask your good caregivers what you can do to thank them (like write a letter to their boss). Maybe pop into your local Target or Walmart store and ask where you can find a Michael Graves Rollator chair.

And as patients, it wouldn't hurt us to think of the world from the provider's "mouse-eye" view, having invested years in training, bearing the daily responsibility for life-and-death decisions, and navigating a rocky landscape now undergoing intense, unprecedented upheaval. Extend a hand by doing your part.

There is no more crucial time for teamwork.

And for all of us using health care, can we teach ourselves, as we teach our children, that we can't have everything we want all the time, without limit? Can we all have real conversations with our families about limiting extraordinary measures to what's meaningful and preferable when that time comes? Can we grasp the inevitable truth that if we want to age in our own homes, we have to take care of some in-house details now, or face having our choices stripped away in a time of crisis? Can we own the consequences of our lifestyle choices—or at the very least, change our mindset that these consequences are other people's problems?

LIVE TO INNOVATE:

Critical Opportunities for Healthcare

1. **Ask staff for ideas.**
2. **Set small, attainable goals.** Success feels good and builds momentum.
3. **Identify "bright spots" and clone them** (the 100,000 Lives Campaign proved peer pressure can be an effective tool. Are there more ways to leverage it?)
4. **"Paint a picture" of your vision.** Use specifics when you share it (as Don Berwick did).
5. **Ask the patient to take initiative in forming goals**
6. **Look for ways to speed up the feedback gap.** Patients who get an instant reading on their glucose levels are less likely to reach for more cake.
7. **Have an idea for a product or service that would improve the delivery of health care?** Perhaps your hospital or hospital system will partner on creating and trialing your innovation, and help distribute it through a mutually beneficial arrangement. Several private companies can also help bring your idea into reality and give you a share of royalties or licensing fees, such as Edison Nation Medical (EdisonNationMedical.com), Eureka Medical (EurekaMed), Sam Medical Products (SamMedical.com), and Xodus Medical (Xodusmedical.com). Also check out a new "crowd-funding" platform, MedStartr.com (it's like Kickstarter.com, but for medical products).

Critical Opportunities for Patients & Families

1. **Speak up!** Add your voice, leave a comment, post a Tweet.
2. **Have an idea for a product or service that would improve the delivery of health care?** Consider submitting your idea to a company that will help bring your idea into reality and give you a split of the profits or licensing fees, like Edison Nation Medical (EdisonNationMedical.com) or Lambert & Lambert, Inc. (LambertInvent.com). Or check out MedStartr.com, a new "crowd-funding" platform for medical products.

"All truth passes through three stages. First, it is ridiculed. Second, it is violently opposed. Third, it is accepted as being self-evident."
—**Arthur Schopenhauer** German philosopher (1788 – 1860)

Final Thoughts

Back in 1950, there were only 3,000 people 100 years old or older on our planet. By 2050, demographers believe there will be more than 6 *million* people over age 100!

What do you want your old age to look like?

My doctor friend David Lowe, MD, who's saved countless lives in the last forty years, recently said he hoped to live his life "like a one-horse shay." *"What the heck is that?"* I asked. He told me it's a two-wheeled carriage drawn by a single horse, built in Maine in the late nineteenth century. It was memorialized in a poem by Oliver Wendell Holmes, Sr. As Dr. Dave explained, the poem is about a deacon who built this wonderful one-horse shay so it wouldn't ever break down. He built it from the very best of materials so that each and every part was as strong as every other part. In Holmes' humorous yet "logical" twist, the shay endures for a hundred years to the day, then it *"went to pieces all at once, and nothing first,—just as bubbles do when they burst…It was built in such a 'logical way' that it ran a hundred years to a day."*

I'd like to be a "one-horse shay," too. On my hundredth birthday, I'd simply collapse while picking tomatoes in my garden. It stinks that it rarely works that way. Unfortunately, our parts wear out. About 25 percent of the money Medicare spends every year is for the last year of life, unchanged from twenty years ago. Slightly more than half of Medicare dollars are spent on patients who die within two months. We know what those last months often look like: dependent, sick, surrounded by unfamiliar people, in a setting where nothing you touch is yours. Focused on illness rather than living. It's how my father lived his last days.

Dr. Dave, now in his sixties, has a cheap prescription for fighting disease and staying out of the hospital (though there are no guarantees). It's one he himself follows faithfully. He runs four miles a day, spends time with family and hobbies, shuns alcohol and tobacco ("they are both carcinogens at any dose—there is no safe amount"), and eats stuff that's good for him. Anger, he adds, is heart-destructive and should be avoided "except when fighting grizzly bears and saber-toothed tigers." He wants people to understand there is a consequence to every medical intervention. Every pill, procedure, and screening comes at the expense of at least one other choice, which is to do nothing. It's good to understand there is always that choice, especially as our bodies reach an age where even a minor complication can launch a downward spiral. When this happens, our family may, with the best of intentions, assert doctors must "do everything" for us, even if we ourselves would prefer something else.

When my time comes, if I'm lucky enough to choose, I hope I can be more like Jack Nicholson in *The Bucket List*. Maybe I too will check myself out of the hospital to skydive and climb mountains. Or maybe I'll just sit at the dinner table with my family, a grandchild on my knee. It's a comforting thought.

I hope health care is in a better place by then.

Pat Mastors
February 2013

Afterword

The hardest part of writing this book was deciding when to end it. Virtually every day I read a new report, gain a new insight or learn from a new contact—at a pace and volume that continues to accelerate. It's tough on publishing deadlines, but gives me hope that change is in the air.

As I sign off on fiddling further with the book, a new wave of tell-all, "insider" books and movies is clamoring for attention. Weeks before the presidential election, the award-winning documentary ESCAPE FIRE: The Fight to Rescue American Healthcare hit theaters. The film about the nation's disastrous state of health care by directors Susan Frömke and Matthew Heineman lit a fire in the patient advocate community, though some media critics found the topic a bit vast and overwhelming. "Surely consumers already know that lobbyists are too influential, drug companies protect their bottom line and insurance companies are out of control," says one reviewer, "... there are neither enough personal histories nor enough proposed solutions to spark any significant debate."[157]

Among the books out in 2012 skewering our dysfunctional health care system: *Overdiagnosed: Making People Sick in the Pursuit of Health; First, Do Less Harm: Confronting the Inconvenient Problems of Patient Safety; How We Do Harm: A Doctor Breaks Ranks About Being Sick in America*; and *Unaccountable: What Hospitals Won't Tell You and How Transparency Can Revolutionize Health Care.*

I have yet to read each of these books, but the one by Marty Makary MD, a cancer surgeon at Johns Hopkins hospital, took me further into the dark, twisted underbelly of medical harm than I'd ever been before. *Unaccountable: What Hospitals Won't Tell You and How Transparency Can Revolutionize Health Care* is a truthful – and terrifying—insider's look at "a medical culture that routinely leaves surgical sponges inside patients, amputates the wrong limbs, and overdoses children because of sloppy handwriting." (Amazon.com review). Maybe it's the Hollywood-quality film trailer that accompanied the book's launch…or the sheer number of the nation's top health care leaders saying how bad things are…or the chilling stories of harm, simply told, by a top-level member of the physicians' inner circle…but this book scared me.

I hope these books and films help wake us patients up. It would be a shame if they become just so many shrieking alarms getting lost in all the noise—a consumer version of the "alarm fatigue" that plagues the very hospitals where harm occurs.

On the plus side:

The federal Partnership for Patients, an initiative from the Department of Health and Human Services, is moving ahead with its challenge to hospitals: to reduce healthcare-acquired conditions by 40 %, and 30-day hospital readmissions by 20%, by the end of 2013. This is a massive undertaking, harnessing the paid help of 26 "hospital engagement networks" (HENs), which in turn are working with member hospitals nationwide. Several times in 2012 and into 2013, I and other patient/family representatives have met with the group leaders and contributed at their workshops. The most recent gathering, on November 30, 2012, saw twenty-one patient/family representatives invited, out of about a hundred total attendees (relative to the prior meeting, where there were six out of one hundred). The one-to-five ratio was remarkable, and led to a robust exchange if ideas, offers of help, and planning. This was followed a couple of weeks later by QualityNet12, where 1,300 people from a range of quality improvement organizations as well as patient/family advocates exchanged information and offers of help. I'm anxious to see how close we can come to the PfP goals in the allotted time, and also wondering what happens what the clock runs out.

Consumers have many more choices today than they did even a few short years ago

From websites where you can rate your doctor or book a same-day medical appointment, to a growing body of professional patient advocates for hire, to new crowd-funding platforms that facilitate bringing innovation to the market—all are good for consumers. The expanding role of Accountable Care Organizations and the patient-centered medical home will continue to shift new opportunity to the private sector. By the time this book is published and in your hands, who knows what new products and services will be available to solve your medical questions and problems? If you have a medical challenge of any kind, type a few key words in a Google search engine. You might be surprised at what's out there.

The first ever "Partnership With Patients" (PWP) Summit (remember reading about organizer Regina Holliday in Chapter 9?) was a resounding success. Organized and funded through the tools of social media, using crowd-funding platforms like Medstartr.com, some 70 patients and providers came together in Kansas City in September 2012 to strategize on when/how/where the patient's voice can and should impact the course of change. We left with new friends in our networks and new strategies on how to make a difference. The three days of the conference yielded two million Twitter impressions (defined as the maximum number of times a link was seen by Twitter users).

The PWP event, with its social media focus, and high-energy, creative events like an "un-conference" (a participant-driven meeting) and a dozen "Ignite" presentations (20 slides, 20 seconds each) offered compelling ideas how providers, policy-makers and patients might work more nimbly and effectively for change.

A draft "common national agenda" for patients and patient advocates, based on input from the September 2012 Partnership With

Patients Summit, has made its first rounds through the blog, Twitter and Facebook world, gathering feedback and suggestions. From the draft: "We who attended saw how exciting it would be through technology and social media to "crowd-source" a focused, common, national patient advocate agenda—taking contributions from the "many" that artfully create a "whole"—an agenda that can be embraced by the widest possible group. Each member of the group would then, by virtue of promoting this agenda, become a designated representative of thousands. The agenda would be a dynamic tool, responsive to the ongoing loop of feedback by its members."

The plan is to distill the agenda from a series of on-line surveys, combined with outreach to communities that aren't served by social media. Outreach to like-minded organizations with the infrastructure to execute will follow. We have high hopes the power of "the many"—especially well-focused power—will make a difference.

The Obama administration is planning to create a first-ever "reporting system for patient safety". A draft questionnaire asks patients to "tell us the name and address of the doctor, nurse or other health care provider involved in the mistake." And it asks patients for permission to share the reports with health care providers "so they can learn about what went wrong and improve safety." No public reporting mechanism like this currently exists. It would be a phenomenal consumer empowerment tool, if it actually launches. There's always the danger that lobbyists and special interests that publicly commend the concept will privately harness their massive resources to torpedo the idea.

If such a system became a reality, as written in our draft "common national agenda" for patients and advocates, I'd like patients and families nationwide (some hospitals already provide this) to have a recourse as they witness a "failure to rescue" unfold before their eyes. From the draft: " I think of advocates like Helen Haskell, and the panic of feeling in real time that you're losing someone you love, and that no one will listen." Imagine a "panic button" on a poster on the walls of every Emergency Room and in each patient's room. It would have a phone app and a toll-free number connected to this reporting database. These reports would be anonymous but you'd have to agree to submit a full report later (to protect the integrity of the results). Maybe each hospital could choose to assign a person who'd pick up on such calls in real time. Or maybe to start, the data just accumulates to flag patterns of harm in particular hospitals, wards or floors.

People-centric initiatives are gaining traction. At the University of California San Francisco, for instance, student interns are trained to accompany patients and their loved ones to medical visits, where they take notes, record discussions and help rehearse the questions the patient/family might want to ask. The service is part of the students' academic training and is free to patients. Both UCSF and Dartmouth report great success with the "Patient Support Corps". Jeff Belkora, Director of Decision Services at UCSF, hopes to roll out the program around the country. More at patientsupportcorps.org.

Medical insiders are "coming out" and pushing for improvement. Marty Makary, MD, for instance, the Hopkins surgeon mentioned above, offers in *Unaccountable* more than a dire overview of a hopeless health care system. He includes promising solutions, all of which invite market forces—the consumer—to drive change. These include

- **Online dashboards**, where every hospital would publicly post its rate of infection, readmission, surgical complication and "never" events, as well as annual volume for each type of surgery it performs and patient satisfaction scores.
- **Safety Culture Scores:** publicly posting the anonymous ratings employees of each hospital give for safety and teamwork. Makary points out these results correlate strongly with infection rates and safety outcomes. He helped institute such a system at Johns Hopkins, and he urges its adoption by all hospitals. (He also recommends patients choose a hospital, when time allows, by asking employees of that hospital if they'd go there themselves.)
- **Cameras: recording events like surgical procedures and hand-washing consistency** to improve compliance with well-established "best practices".
- **Open Notes:** giving patients access to the notes their doctors write about you, and even being allowed to add your own comments. This ensures accuracy and promotes teamwork. (A landmark report

published October 1, 2012 in the Annals of Internal Medicine indicates "Open Notes" are a winner for both patients and doctors. The study funded by the Robert Wood Johnson Foundation looked at hospitals across a variety of settings, surveying over 100 docs and nearly 20,000 patients. Nearly 99 percent of patients wanted to continue with Open Notes, and no physician elected to stop. In addition, doctors in the study reported more than half of patients who received medication improved adherence.[158])

- **No More Gagging:** Patients continue to be asked to sign a gag order, promising not to say anything negative about their doctor. Gag orders have also long been the price a patient has paid to get any kind of settlement compensation in a medical lawsuit.

The government's role, Makary asserts, is to insist the above measures boost transparency, trust and accountability.

Patient Advocates Are Gaining Access. A 2011 federal mandate requires hospitals that treat Medicare and Medicaid patients to maximize support for them, by allowing access to family, friends, and designated visitors. This has more hospitals nationwide rolling out new visitation policies that allow round-the-clock visits, and permits patients to choose a support person who can stay with them overnight.

The First Clinical Proof Fecal Transplants Can Cure *C.diff* came out in January 2013. A new study out of the Netherlands published January 2013 in *The New England Journal of Medicine* finds that such transplants cured 15 of 16 people who had recurring infections with *Clostridium difficile* bacteria. In two comparison groups, antibiotics cured only 3 of 13 and 4 of 13 patients. Many of the public comments to the various media reports were from *C.diff* sufferers (or their families) who had tried everything before finally finding this simple, inexpensive and effective treatment.

Social Media is Helping "Connect the Dots". I continue to stumble over accomplished, committed groups that don't necessarily know about each other—like Healthcare Innovation by Design (HIxD), www.healthcareinnovationbydesign.com. More than 5,000 members gather virtually for webinars, networking and career opportunities. Says founder Sam Basta MD, an internist with Sentara Healthcare in Norfolk,

Virginia, "members are clinicians, designers, architects, engineers and IT professionals from elite US and international healthcare organizations and centers of innovation." Until I told him, Basta had not heard about Ben Miller or the fledgling OccupyHealthcare.net. Combining forces, resources and agendas may not be easy, but it's easier if we all know about each other.

The Society for Participatory Medicine, a sponsor of the September Partnership with Patients Summit, is monitoring and promoting these historic changes in health care as much as any group. It's a bunch of brilliant thinkers, very generous with their insights. It was at the PWP Summit that I met the group's president-elect, a man whose writing I had long admired, and who understands this transformational time in our history better than most.

Michael L. Millenson is president of his own Health Quality consulting firm and a nationally recognized expert on improving the quality of American health care. He sounded the alarm for quality and accountability as far back as 2000 in his critically acclaimed book, *Demanding Medical Excellence: Doctors and Accountability in the Information Age*. He lectures at the Harvard Business School and the Institute for Healthcare Improvement, and his byline is on many articles published in *USA Today, the Washington Post* and the *British Medical Journal*. I asked Michael for his long view of the patient safety movement and the road ahead. The words below are his.

The modern patient safety movement began with a newspaper story that stunned the nation's medical elite. In early 1995, the Boston Globe told how their medical writer, Betsy Lehman, had been killed by a massive chemotherapy overdose a few months earlier at a Harvard-affiliated hospital that was one of the most respected in the nation.[159] It was also a place where the husband of the 39-year old mother of two worked as a research scientist. Their complaints that something just wasn't right were ignored.

As U.S. News and World Report put it:

"[T]he irony that a renowned hospital failed perhaps the quintessential well-informed patient still resonates – with other patients, as well as within the walls of Dana-Farber [Cancer Institute].[160]

That question Lehman's death raised still haunts us: what can well-informed patients do to protect themselves and their loved ones from harm?

As this book has shown, being an active, informed and involved patient can be critical. Still, our actions as patients can only reduce the chances of harm, not eliminate them. Yes, you can refuse the red pill because you know it should be blue, nag the nurses to wash their hands and use the tools and insights recommended in this book. But those who are in charge of treatment still must respond. Moreover, in a world of complex medications and medical procedures, we depend even more heavily upon doctors and hospitals practicing safe care in the first place.

Lehman's death prompted profound change at Dana-Farber. A Globe article ten years after Lehman's death called it "one of the most safety-conscious hospitals in America."[161] Patient safety became "a core property of our system of care rather than an empty mantra," two of its leaders later related. "We decided that patient safety was and is the work of the organization, not an activity that could be compartmentalized."[162]

Dana-Farber's innovations included an unprecedented partnering with patients. The hospital not only instituted patient and family advisory councils; patient and family representatives sit on major decision-making bodies throughout the institution. This is truly participatory medicine "from the exam room to the boardroom."

Unfortunately, Dana-Farber's commitment has been far from universally copied. A 2010 study found that the Institute of Medicine's famed 1999 report on up to 98,000 preventable hospital deaths care had not prompted hospital care nationally to improve significantly.[163] While there are more providers than ever actively committed to eliminating patient harm, powerful barriers still stand in the way. [164]

What can we as individuals do? First, activism as patients remains important even if the impact is not always obvious. In the summer of 2011, a bicycle accident left my wife with a broken bone in her left arm and a small fracture of the C-1 vertebra that required her head to be immediately stabilized. She was treated at a small hospital in Maine, a major teaching hospital in Boston and then a big community hospital in suburban Chicago, near our home.

I have no direct evidence that my constant involvement helped keep her safe. However, I am certain that the depth and breadth of my questions left an impression with front-line staff, as did my follow-up letter thanking all three hospital administrators for their institution's safety awareness.[165] Although providers may not always explicitly acknowledge it, we are critical partners in building a safety culture.

Just as important is how we act as citizens. Hospitals and doctors do not rush to embrace transparency and accountability for their actions any more than the rest of us do. In an era of intense discussion about the proper role of government, it's important to support modest programs like the Health Engagement Networks that promise outsized results in terms of lives and even money saved. One recent study put the cost of the toll taken on individuals and families by medical errors at $73.5 billion to $98 billion in "quality-adjusted life years."[166]

Finally, we need to make patient safety part of our home and work communities. We do so by talking with friends, neighbors, colleagues, personal physicians and others in a way that summons a sense of our common values. At the beginning of this book, Pat reminds us of the personal loss and love that motivated that. We need to hold fast to that emotional truth. We cannot let the numbers numb us, or the magnitude of the task deter us.

As Betsy Lehman's mother, Mildred, wrote: "Patient safety must be utmost and constant, both ingrained into the system…and into caring hearts."

"Our lives begin to end the day we become silent about things that matter."

—Martin Luther King, Jr.

Resources

1. The Author's Tips for a Better Hospital Stay
2. Trisha Torrey's Tips on Being an Empowered Patient
3. Online Resources from The Empowered Patient Coalition
4. What Frustrates Physicians about Us Patients
5. Cynthia Leibrock's Tips for Aging in Place (and in Control)

Over the years I've gathered tips to help patients from numerous sources. I hope the list below helps. I also encourage you to do your own independent research.[167]

Pat Mastors' Tips for a Better Hospital Stay

1. **If you have the option, choose your hospital carefully.** Check out hospital "report cards" at the Leapfrog Group's www.hospitalsafetyscore.org. However your best information might come from asking nurses, doctors and other staff what hospital they'd go to for that procedure.

2. **While hospitalized, appoint a companion if possible.** Having a friend or relative with you can be important the first night after surgery and at times you are too sick to speak for yourself. If the companion can perform simple tasks—like tidy the bed—it will free up the nurses for more sophisticated patient care. When you call on your nurses, they'll know it's important and you'll find them appreciative.

3. **Pack for safety as well as comfort.** Bring hand sanitizer for your bedside, use it often, and make sure it doesn't get moved out of reach. Pack a notepad and pen and take notes (or ask your advocate to do this for you). Bring your cell phone, charger and an extension cord. Make sure you drink lots of water before, during and after your hospitalization. Good hydration is important for healing. Bring your own non-skid slippers if you can.

4. **In the hospital setting, it is especially important to wash your hands before eating, and to avoid touching your mouth or nose with unclean hands.** *Clostridium difficile* or *C. diff* is a bacteria carried by some of us in our digestive systems. *C. diff* (along with certain other infectious germs) can also gain access into our body when we touch an object (a table or bed rail, for example) that was not thoroughly cleaned, and then touch our mouth or nose. *C. diff* often won't cause problems until you begin to take antibiotics for another illness. This can kill off certain kinds of intestinal bacteria, allowing *C. diff* bacteria to grow out of control, making you very ill. (Hand washing, rather than alcohol gels, is effective in eliminating *C. diff*...the running water actually flushes the spoors down the drain.) If you have been taking an antibiotic, be aware that the first sign of *C. diff* infection is usually nausea and vomiting. Keep purses, briefcases, and backpacks (whose bottoms carry large amounts of fecal bacteria) off beds and tables. If something falls on the floor, never put it back on the bed, bed table, or chair.

5. **As an extra measure of precaution, consider bringing a tub of antimicrobial wipes** and wipe down all surfaces you're likely to touch (bed rails, bed table, remote control, phone, etc.), to guard against infection. Be sensitive to the staff and explain it's

no reflection on their cleaning practices, you just want to be extra cautious. Consider bleach wipes, which are effective against any *C.diff* spores left behind from another patient. Wipe these surfaces fairly often, especially if many people are touching them. Make sure you use hospital gloves when handling hospital-grade wipes.

6. **Insist on cleanliness.** It can feel awkward to ask your visitor, doctor, or nurse to wash their hands and/or use gloves before touching you, but good hand hygiene is the best way to avoid infection in the hospital. (If you have your own bottle of hand sanitizer, you can offer someone approaching you a squirt, which is less awkward than sending them back to the dispenser in the doorway.) Use your knuckles to press elevator buttons.

7. **Be alert for how infections are transmitted.** Germs, such as MRSA, enter the skin through surgical wounds or intravenous (IV) lines inserted into your body to deliver drugs, fluids, or nutrition. Any break in the skin is a potential "port of entry" for infection. If the skin around a surgical wound, intravenous line, or catheter should become red, swollen, hot, or painful, or if you develop chills or feel feverish, alert hospital staff immediately.

8. **Be aware of "the thin brown line,"** as one infection-control expert says. Many germs—including tough-to-get-rid-of *C. diff*—are transmitted via trace amounts of feces. Are the people emptying your bedpan grabbing the privacy curtain afterward? Or bringing your food tray? This is a great time to gently ask that they clean their hands in between to keep these surfaces clean. Also, visitors *should not* use patients' bathrooms.

9. **Write down developments,** medications administered, names of procedures, instructions given, and dates and times of the above (your advocate can do this for you, too). Ask and record the names of caregivers, and understand the hierarchy so you know who's in charge and whom to speak to if there's a problem. Attitude is important—you're just trying to be a cooperative and collaborative partner!. Also jot down any questions as they occur to you, so you won't forget them when the caregiver enters your room. If you have a special need (like an allergy or hearing problem), post a

big note over the bedside and other spots they're likely to be seen. Keep notes, handouts, and discharge information organized in a folder or clean container—these will be your guide and reference point once you leave the hospital. (If you have a Patient Pod, you can post a note in the pear-shaped message clip, and you can store your papers inside the Pod.) Consider opening an account at CaringBridge.org, which lets you, share updates with friends and family and also stands as your record of events.

10. **Be polite but assertive when necessary.** Complaining too often or too aggressively about minor inconveniences can alienate the multi-tasking staff. But you should expect reasonable and timely responses to reasonable requests and questions. If you're being neglected, ask to speak to the hospital's patient advocate or social-service worker.

11. **Patients with intravenous (IV) fluids or medications should make sure the IV is inserted and removed under clean conditions.** Your skin should be cleaned at the site of insertion (with the sterilizing liquid wiped on you allowed to dry first), and the person treating you should be wearing clean gloves. Safe care dictates that an IV (intravenous line) should be changed every two to three days to control the risk of infection at the site—sooner if the IV was inserted under emergency conditions. An IV in the femoral artery (groin area) is especially prone to infection.

12. **Do not shave the surgical site.** Razors can create small nicks in the skin, through which bacteria can enter. If hair must be removed before surgery, use clippers or ask that clippers be used instead of a razor.[2] (Women—don't shave your body at all before surgery! One doctor friend tells me shaving ourselves "smooth" in a desire to look "well-groomed" while under the knife is just about the dumbest thing we can do. If you must shave, use an electric razor.)

13. **Since tests show one-third of blood pressure cuffs** on carts rolled from room to room had *C. diff* bacteria on the inside, inquire if a new cuff can be dedicated to your use and left in your room.

14. **Ask about minimizing use of a urinary tract catheter.** These catheters have been a common cause of infection. The tube

carries urine from your bladder out of your body. After 48 hours of catheterization, most catheters are colonized with bacteria, thus leading to possible infection and its complications. If you have a catheter, ask your caregiver if it can be removed as soon as possible.

15. **Don't add to the problem.** Everything you touch in the hospital, from magazines, to elevator buttons, to your clothing and purse, can carry potentially deadly germs to the next hospital surface you touch (cafeteria food, ATM machine, etc.) Don't pass along your loved one's used newspaper or magazines to other patients. And be faithful about using contact precautions like wearing gowns and gloves if you're asked.

16. **Bringing your cell phone along? Don't forget to clean it.** When researchers tested 25 cell phones, 20 percent came up positive for MRSA. And remember, while you're in the hospital, others may "helpfully" answer your calls or move your cell phone. Sanitize your cell with a disinfecting wipe.

17. **Do not walk on the floor in bare feet** for all the reasons stated above. Wear slippers and clean hands after touching them.

18. **Be nice! Make friends with your nurses, phlebotomists (people who draw blood) and other hospital personnel.** Make sure they address you by name at least once each shift.[168]

19. **Before you are given a medication, a transfusion, an X-ray or a procedure, make sure the nurse confirms your name both by asking and checking your wristband.**

20. **Before being taken off the floor for a procedure, ask what it is and be sure you understand where you are going and why.**

21. **Be sure your family members' contact information is available** to the hospital or nursing home personnel (it's not a bad idea to place a card with your family's contact information by your bedside or posted prominently—in addition to being sure that this information is on the chart).

22. **Before being transferred from floor-to-floor** in a hospital (such as an ICU to the general medical or surgical floor) or from one institution to another, check to be sure all catheters and other

paraphernalia that should be removed have been (sometimes caregivers will forget to remove an IV line or urinary catheter before a transfer, which creates an unnecessary risk of infection).

23. **Read up on** *C.diff,* **a growing and dangerous threat inside and outside the hospital.** Check sites like WebMD and the websites of the CDC and the Mayo Clinic. The Peggy Lillis Memorial Foundation (PeggyFoundation.org) offers wonderful resources, advocacy and community.

Trisha Torrey's Tips on Being an Empowered Patient

Trisha Torrey, an author, blogger, and consultant who runs several online resources for patients and their advocates, offers these patient empowerment tips:

1. Become an expert in your own medical challenges. Read everything you can, ask questions, study anatomy, acquire and review copies of all your medical records. Be the authority on YOU.

2. Using your self-authority, partner with your doctors and other providers. While they may have the education and experience, you've lived in your body your entire life. If your provider won't listen and share in your decision-making, then find one who will.

3. Pursue a second opinion whenever you are diagnosed with a difficult disease or condition, or when surgery, chemo, or long-term treatment is prescribed.

4. Don't be afraid to say NO. Sometimes less is more. As the authority on YOU, you'll know when NO is the right answer.

5. Thank your doctors and staff members when they have been collaborative and helpful. They work in a tough environment. Appreciation, when appropriate, can go a long way.

6. Read and listen past the headlines. Get the whole story, and then pursue additional, objective sources. In particular, be sure Internet information is credible.

7. Review your medical bills. Experts tell us that up to 80 percent of medical bills contain errors. Incorrect bills will eventually cost us all in higher premiums and taxes.

8. Provide support to others. Shared experiences can help others who suffer the same medical challenges you do. Refer them to good doctors and good resources.

9. Accept support from others. Whether it's a loved one or a professional, sometimes it's imperative to have an advocate by your side.

10. Finally, wash your hands regularly and cough or sneeze into your elbow. Infections are dangerous and deadly whether acquired during a hospital stay or brought home from school by the kids. Hygiene can go a long way toward keeping infection at bay.

Online Resources from the Empowered Patient Coalition

Julia Hallisy founded carefully vetted online resource www.empoweredpatientcoalition.org. Julia, a dentist, lost her daughter Kate after an eight-year battle with a rare cancer of the eye and spent those years navigating and learning about how to get the best medical care. Check the website for the most updated "resources for the well-informed patient."

What Frustrates Physicians about Us Patients

1. **Meddling families in the room.**[169] About 16 percent of all patients bring a companion—a spouse, adult child, parent, or friend—to their doctor's appointments.[170] While this second set of eyes and ears can be critical, the crowd can sometimes interfere with a doctor's work or a patient's well-being. "You get a husband and wife in a room and one is overweight and one of them is not, and the other starts saying, 'See, I told you so,'" said one New York physician. Such distractions may impede the doctor's ability to communicate, or the patient's ability to discuss his or her symptoms.

2. **Demanding a drug they saw "on TV."** The United States is one of the few countries in the world that allows direct-to-consumer drug advertising. Since the FDA's 1997 decision to let drug companies market pharmaceuticals to the masses (previous drug marketing was aimed largely at physicians), doctors have reported more patients asking about specific drugs than ever before.

3. **Quitting medication without notice.** Physicians are frustrated when patients discontinue medications because of adverse reactions or expense—but don't let them know about it until they come in with problems again.

4. **Demanding tests and procedures.** "This is the bias some patients have to just doing more, without any understanding of how more care is not only expensive, but actually often leads to complications, poor outcomes, and lower quality," says Dr. Thomas Schwenk, chairman of family medicine at the University of Michigan.

5. **Lawsuits.** While some lawsuits are justified and fair, others are not. Fear of litigation can also drive doctors to over test and over treat, as we saw with an extreme and frightening example in chapter 6.

6. **Judging with incomplete information.** With data like physician ratings, hospital infections rates, and patient satisfaction scores making their way to public reporting websites, providers are a little skittish about how we patients will interpret what we see—especially when key information is left out.

Cynthia Leibrock's Tips for Aging in Place (and in Control)

1. Tape down rugs (a tripping hazard).

2. Add handrails with extensions to both sides of stairs.

3. Add grab bars to your shower (Hafele makes some, which can snap on when needed, and there are nice choices at http://www.greatgrabz.com/.

4. Add offset pivot hinges to narrow doors. (The door takes up two inches of space in the frame when it's open. These hinges pivot the door out of the frame, gaining 2 inches of clearance.)

5. Replace your showerhead with a handheld shower on a vertical grab bar.

6. If you have trouble hearing on your phone, replace it with one that amplifies high frequencies, not one that just increases the volume (Ameriphone sells several models for $100 or less).

7. Put a non-slip finish on your wood floors (Bona offers a good non-slip finish).

8. For bathroom floors, consider wood or unglazed ceramic tile with recessed area rugs (instead of bath mats). The area rugs can be removed and cleaned.

9. Use a "drop-down bottom" on a door instead of a threshold, which is a tripping hazard. It's a rubber seal in a thin metal frame that sits on the bottom of the door. It has a small button on the side, which compresses when the door is closed. This drops the seal to a tight fit on the floor and raises it again when you open the door. (Cynthia says almost all door suppliers carry this.)

10. Install an induction cook top to avoid burns and fires. Almost all manufacturers have one these days. Portable models can sometimes be found on Amazon.com or Overstock.com for less than $200. Whirlpool has a built-in for less than $1000.

11. Consider installing a side-hinged oven. Fagor sells one for less than $1000.

12. When replacing your washer/dryer, buy front-loading models, and elevate them by adding built-in drawers below. Remove the drawers for easy use from a wheelchair.

13. For showers, says Cynthia, "I usually don't use shower doors in a universal bathroom. It's hard to maneuver around them with a mobility device. The best shower uses a trench drain with a cover at floor height. Collapsible thresholds and gaskets hold the water in, but they are tripping hazards. If the shower is large enough, you don't even need a shower curtain. In smaller showers, use a curtain that touches the floor and is held there with a chain weight in the hem.

Live long and well!

—**Pat**

Acknowledgments

Many thanks to my fellow patient advocates, some of the most tireless and committed people I know. You amaze me with your inspiring drive to create positive change out of devastating loss. Special thanks to my dear friend Patty Skolnik for your generous spirit and inviting me to help spread the message. Thanks to Dave deBronkart and Regina Holliday for blazing the trail in compelling and colorful ways. Thanks to Helen Haskell for that first connection, and to Ilene Corina for all you do to bring comfort to the bedside. For so generously sharing your stories, and all you do for patients, thanks to Alicia Cole, Kathy Day, Rosemary Gibson, Julia Hallisy, John James, Linda Kenney, Christian John Lillis, Mary Ellen Mannix, Dale Ann Micalizzi, Bob Oshel, Jean Rexford, Trisha Torrey and every one of you who answered a question and offered help. At Consumer's Union Safe Patient Project, thanks to Lisa McGiffert, Daniela Nunez, and Suzanne Henry. To my young friend Emily Croke, your Dad would be so proud of you and your award-winning video, "A Silent Epidemic". You're reaching a whole new generation with the patient safety message, and that's critical.

To those who tend us at the bedside, thank you for knowing the power of a kind touch and encouraging smile, and for using it, especially when we patients are at our most cranky and miserable. You are angels on earth.

To physicians who've sacrificed and invested so much so that you can heal us, thank you from the bottom of my heart. New software, therapies, and tech tools may increasingly crowd the landscape, but we will always need your trained mind and skilled hands. Yes, we look up to you. I hope you're always as awed and humbled as we are by the miracles you help create. We need you to keep inspiring little boys and girls to follow in your footsteps. A special shout-out to David Lowe and Stefan Gravenstein.

To Michael Graves, your courage is humbling, and your mission is inspiring. In the face of a loss that might have crushed your spirit, you re-thought the design of your life, and are using it as a platform to right what's wrong. Thank you for bringing beauty, simplicity and dignity to the world of the patient, and a more sensible environment to those who care for them.

A zillion people helped me in ways large and small. Thanks to Joe Amaral, MD, for insights from the C-suite, and for convincing me early on I could make a difference. Thanks to Joe Cacciola, Wayne Blatchley (and the entire Fuzion Design team), Judy Hager, Kathleen Bajo, Peg Fradette, and Aimee Keenan-Greene. Marty Hatlie, thanks for helping draw the fine line. Sandy Coletta, you have the heart and vision of a true leader. Thanks to Rep. Eileen Naughton, who submitted our two patient safety measures to the RI legislature, and saw them through to passage. For insights and support, thanks to Cindy Leibrock, Peter Lambert, Tim McDonald, Ben Miller, and Michael Millenson. To David Hancock, Margo Toulouse, Rick Frishman, Bethany Marshall, Bonnie Bushman and the entire publishing and design team at Morgan James, thanks for helping to get this book out into the world. Amanda Rooker, your red pen made it better. Michael Graves, Dounia Tamri-Loeper and Salvatore Forgione, thanks for the teamwork it took to make the outside of the book reflect the urgency and attention that went into it. To Wendy Lipton-Dibner, thanks for helping me find my voice.

Thanks to my Mom, brothers, and circle of "sisters": Katie, Mac, Suz, and Kathy, and for my "third daughter" Molly who teaches us all so much. Last, writing a book takes tremendous time and energy, and sometimes skipping opportunities to be with the people you love most. To Nick, Jess, and Elizabeth, thanks for your cheering and support. Watching you reach high for your own goals makes me believe anything is possible! To my wonderful husband, Jim—your insights and tough questions made me think. Your unwavering support made it possible. And your caring heart told me it mattered. Thank you for being the shepherd and cheerleader of dreams.

About the Author

Pat Mastors, a longtime news and medical reporter, began her work in patient advocacy following the death of the father in the hospital. She lobbied successfully to pass new patient safety laws in Rhode Island and works on a state and national level to improve patient safety. She is creator of the "Patient Pod", a bedside device to improve the patient's safety and communication. She presents frequently to community, medical and industry groups on enhancing patient safety and engagement. Pat and her husband live in Rhode Island and are the parents of two daughters and a son. *Design to Survive: 9 Ways An IKEA Approach Can Fix Health Care & Save Lives* is her first book.

Endnotes

1   Various studies point to a range numbers of how many are killed or hurt by medical harm, and of those, how many deaths are preventable. Michael Millenson, a Chicago-based consultant who writes extensively about health care, lays out an excellent examination of these numbers in a Health Affairs blog post (March 9, 2012) at http://healthaffairs.org/blog/2012/03/09/the-toll-of-preventable-errors-how-many-dead-patients/.

2   "More Than One in Four Medicare Beneficiaries Experience Some Degree of Harm While Hospitalized", https://oig.hhs.gov/newsroom/spotlight/2012/adverse.asp.

3   Marty Makary, MD, "How to Stop Hospitals from Killing Us", *Wall Street Journal*, September 21, 2012, http://online.wsj.com/article/SB10000872396390444620104578008263334441352.html.

4   Said James in an email to the author on November 1, 2012 "Health care adds somewhere between 3.5 and 7 years of life expectancy, on average, for every member of U.S. society - a huge total net benefit. The evidence for this is quite strong. Any person would be an idiot, on the evidence, to avoid the health care delivery system because of associated injury rates."

5   U.S. Centers for Disease Control.

6   "Q: What Scares Doctors? A: Being a Patient," *Time Magazine*, April 23, 2006, http://www.time.com/time/magazine/article/0,9171,1186553-1,00.html.

7   Email to author, November 1, 2012.

8   "The IKEA Effect: When Labor Leads to Love", Michael I. Norton, Harvard Business Review, February 2009, p. 30.

9   "Doctor's Orders: Don't Stay Alone in the Hospital," Bigthink.com, January 19, 2010.

10 Steve Sternberg, "Medical Errors Harm Huge Number of Patients", huffintonpost.com, August 29, 2012, http://www.huffingtonpost.com/2012/08/29/medical-errors-hospitals-harm-patients_n_1839814.html.

11 Technically, Kamprad and his family do not own IKEA. In 1982, Kamprad founded Stichting INGKA as a charitable Dutch foundation intended to revolutionize architecture and interior design. Kamprad donated 100 percent of the equity in his company to the foundation, which not only relinquished his ownership of IKEA but also created the world's biggest charity, surpassing even the Bill and Melinda Gates Foundation. Still, Kamprad asserts that he retains the title of Senior Advisor for the company. Since Stichting INGKA is considered a Dutch charity, it is not required to pay taxes even for the revenue gained from the IKEA business.

12 "Television Remote Control Is Leading Carrier of Bacteria in Patient's Hospital Room—New Study out of the University of Arizona," http://www.prnewswire.com/news-releases/television-remote-control-is-leading-carrier-of-bacteria-in-patients-hospital-room—new-study-out-of-the-university-of-arizona-55416657.html.

13 For patients, the cost of an HAI is high; the length of the hospital stay increases by 7-9 days, and they pay $40,000 more on average. For the healthcare system as a whole, HAIs add between $4.5 and $5.7 billion each year. Source" National Patient Safety Foundation (NPSF.org), http://www.npsf.org/for-healthcare-professionals/resource-center/definitions-and-hot-topics/.

14 The Joint Commission, the federal agency that accredits hospitals, has since announced that it will make hospital hygiene and infection prevention a focus of future inspections. But even when such a program is up and running, the risk of harm from contact with an unclean environment will always be there.

15 Around 2004, a new and much more powerful strain of C. diff began showing up in US hospital and nursing-home patients. This strain

releases toxins into the intestine at a rate seventeen-times faster than that of the strain previously known.

16 In May 2012, now-twenty-two-year-old Emily Croke produced a film on hospital-acquired infections that won the Providence College film festival. I was proud to be in the audience to screen the film and watch her receive her award. She hopes to bring the film and topic to national attention.

17 Email to the author, Tuesday, February 5, 2013.

18 "From Tears to Transparency—The Story of Michael Skolnik" debuted in October 2010. It is a project of Transparent Health (Transparenthealth.com) and is shown at patient safety events.

19 http://www.aliciacole.com/My_Story.htm.

20 http://www.aliciacole.com/My_Story.htm.

21 Ilene later had a second healthy child, and then a son Matthew born prematurely at one pound, seven ounces. Ilene credits great teamwork, and the extraordinary support and compassion of caregivers, for the fact that Matthew today is a healthy, happy young man, with only the scars from IV lines to show for his ordeal. Ilene later founded PULSE of NY (Persons United Limiting Substandards and Errors in Healthcare) and today conducts patient-advocacy training workshops. She's a board member of the National Patient Safety Foundation and serves on the Joint Commission on Accreditation of Healthcare Organizations (JCAHO).

22 Today there are more resources to help people develop and manufacture a medical innovation. See "Critical Moves" for providers and patients at the end of Chapter 9.

23 I truly believe when we get to know someone, we begin to care more for them—and that less harm will occur in hospitals when we do a better job of humanizing patients. The care team will respond differently when they know "the hip replacement in 302-B" hopes to be well enough to walk down the aisle at his granddaughter's wedding.

24 To date, the Patient Pod has helped patients throughout the United States and as far away as South Africa. It's distributed by physician practices and through several patient advocacy organizations, will

serve as a critical tool during clinical trials as an adjunct to "teach-back" to reduce 30-day readmission rates at an Ohio hospital system, and will be used in care management of developmentally disabled adults through as part of a recently awarded $14 million Medicare Innovation grant to the University of Rhode Island. The Patient Pod is available online at thePatientPod.com.

25　See　http://www.telegraph.co.uk/health/healthnews/9147414/Resistance-to-antibiotics-could-bring-the-end-of-modern-medicine-as-we-know-it-WHO-claim.html, March 16, 2012.

26　Vanessa G. Allen, MD, MPH; Leo Mitterni; Christine Seah, MLT; Anuradha Rebbapragada, PhD; Irene E. Martin, BSc; Colin Lee, MD; Heather Siebert, MLT; Lynn Towns, MLT; Roberto G. Melano, PhD; Donald E. Low, MD, *Neisseria gonorrhoeae* Treatment Failure and Susceptibility to Cefixime in Toronto, Canada, *Journal of the American Medical Association*, January 9, 2013, Vol 309, No. 2.

27　In response to these concerns, the Food and Drug Administration announced in April 2012 that farmers and ranchers can no longer feed antibiotics to cattle, pigs, chickens, and other animals as a pre-emptive measure. They will now have to get a prescription from a veterinarian before using antibiotics on farm animals.

28　Phage therapy (using viruses to invade bacteria, which destroys them) offers promise of controlling infection with less side effects, but it's only approved in the Soviet country of Georgia. The main barrier to phage's introduction in the West is a lack of published research on the subject in English, the general reliability (until recently) of antibiotics, and the lack of profit for drug companies. Colloidal silver and homeopathic remedies have also been successful in some applications. Further research is needed here, too.

29　*Pseudomonas aeruginosa* is a bacteria that lives in soil, water, and even in environments like hot tubs. For most healthy people, this bacteria seldom poses a problem. Unfortunately, *Pseudomonas aeruginosa* is much more dangerous to certain populations, including those who have weak immune systems, the elderly, and those who have been hospitalized for long periods of time.

30 *Klebsiella,* normally found in the human intestine (where they do not cause disease) can cause different types of healthcare-associated infections, including pneumonia, bloodstream infections, wound or surgical site infections, and meningitis.

31 Andrew Pollack, "Rising Threat of Infections Unfazed by Antibiotics," *New York Times,* February 26, 2010.

32 In April 2012, the Department of Health and Human Services reported central line-associated bloodstream infections had been cut by 33 percent, surgical site infections by 10 percent, catheter-associated urinary tract infections by 7 percent, and invasive MRSA infections by 18 percent (this is compared to record-high numbers).

33 Six years after my father's death, the *C. diff* problem is worse than ever. A front-page *USA Today* investigation published August 16, 2012, entitled "Far More Could Be Done to Stop the Deadly Bacteria *C. diff*" by Peter Eisler "...shows that *C. diff* is far more prevalent than federal reports suggest. The bacteria is linked in hospital records to more than 30,000 deaths a year in the United States— about twice federal estimates and rivaling the 32,000 killed in traffic accidents. It strikes about a half-million Americans a year. "Yet despite a decade of rising *C. diff* rates, health care providers and the government agencies that oversee them have been slow to adopt proven strategies to reduce the infections, resulting in tens of thousands of deaths and illnesses that could have been prevented, the investigation shows."

34 A January 2011 study published in the *Archives of Pediatrics & Adolescent Medicine* says the number of hospitalized children infected by *Clostridium difficile* rose nearly 15 percent a year during the time period studied, 1997 to 2006.

35 After an outbreak of *C. diff* in twenty birthing mothers on the obstetrical service at the University of Washington Medical Center (UWMC) between April 2006 and June 2007, it was concluded that peripartum women appear to be another population susceptible to CDI [*Clostridium Difficile* Infection]. As reported in *Infectious Diseases in Obstetrics and Gynecology* (July 2011), "Hospital obstetrical units pose a unique opportunity for infection control. The environment... provides ample reservoirs and transmission modes for *C. difficile*

infections. Providers have frequent contact with fecal contents during a delivery and travel from one patient room to another in the labor and delivery unit. In these high volume units, rooms are quickly cleaned for reuse, and infectious disease recognition can be neglected…Great vigilance must be taken on multiple levels to decrease the exposure of patients to antibiotic harm and to vigorously work to identify and prevent outbreaks of CDI."

36 According to the National Institutes of Health, "Growing evidence now suggests that community-acquired *Clostridium difficile* infection may account for more than a third of *Clostridium difficile*-associated diarrhea overall. Similar to nosocomial [hospital-acquired] *Clostridium difficile* infection, community-acquired cases appear to be increasing in incidence, and although associated mortality is lower than in nosocomial cases, morbidity including hospitalization and recurrence are high." http://www.ncbi.nlm.nih.gov/pubmed/22218031, January 2012.

37 A 2009 study published by the National Institutes of Health concluded hydrogen peroxide dry-mist disinfection was significantly more effective than bleach at eradicating *C. diff* spores, showing "a decrease in contamination of 50 percent after hypochlorite (bleach) decontamination and 91 percent after hydrogen peroxide decontamination." I inquired of a top infection-control specialist why the less-corrosive hydrogen peroxide alternative was not being pursued more aggressively. His response: "the technology has potential, but also has a number of associated issues making it less amenable to use in the frenetic hospital environment." According to the citation he attached, this would include the need to pre-clean surfaces before the mist is applied, which is labor- and cost-intensive. More on this in chapter 8.

38 A successful therapy is to treat *C. diff* with fecal transplants: stool from a healthy donor is delivered like a suppository to an infected patient, with "good" bacteria in the stool establishing themselves in the gut and beginning to compete with *C. diff*. In 2012, as reported in "Tending the Body's Microbial Garden" (Carl Zimmer, *NY Times,* June 18, 2012), researchers at the University of Alberta reviewed 124

fecal transplants and concluded that the procedure is safe and effective, with 83 percent of patients experiencing immediate improvement as their internal ecosystems were restored. Dr. Alexander Khoruts of the University of Minnesota and his colleagues want to make fecal transplants standard practice. They can now extract bacteria from stool, "removing the 'ick' factor," as he puts it.

39   "One Bacteria, 30,000 Deaths," *USA Today*, August 16, 2012.

40   The end of reimbursement for "never events" was supposed to compel better adherence to best practices and reduce medical harm. However, one internationally respected infection-control colleague confided to me recently these penalties are "less of a big stick and more like a twig." Says he: "We just don't have good data in the first place to prove how much money these events are costing our hospitals—or how much we could save by stopping them."

41   In March 2012, Berwick took a post as a fellow at the Center for American Progress, a Washington think tank. As of January 2013 he was considering a run for governor of Massachusetts.

42   Today, five years post-surgery and treatment, Dave is thriving, so much so that I can barely keep up with his brisk pace as we run to catch a cab in Manhattan. He'll tell you that, for him, the medical system worked flawlessly; he had the right doctors, the right hospital, the right surgery, and the right follow-up treatment, and as an early and smart user of information technology, he participated proactively in the process all along.

43   Tom Ferguson, "e-Patients—How They Can Help Us Heal Health Care," e-Patients white paper, e-patients.net/e-Patients_White_Paper.pdf, March 2007.

44   In February 2012, patient advocate Sue Sheridan became Deputy Director of Patient Engagement at PCORI, a nonprofit organization created by Congress to help patients and those who care for them make better-informed health care decisions. Sheridan became involved in patient safety after her family experienced two medical system failures: Her husband, Pat, died in 2002 after his diagnosis of cancer failed to be communicated. And her son, Cal, suffered a type

of brain damage called kernicterus five days after his birth in 1995 when his neonatal jaundice was untreated.

The much-touted Partnership for Patients (PfP) is a public-private partnership launched by the federal government in 2011 to improve patient safety, increase the quality of care, and lower costs. It's a promising foray into a more formalized, collaborative relationship with patients. I'm honored to be among those contributing ideas surrounding patient-family engagement.

45   Robert M. Wachter, MD, *Understanding Patient Safety* (McGraw-Hill Medical, 2008), 232. (The second edition of *Understanding Patient Safety* was published in May 2012 and is available on Amazon.com.)

46   Via email from IKEA, August 10, 2012.

47   Sean Poulter, "This Flatpack Nation: Ten per Cent of all Furniture Bought by UK Householders Is from IKEA," *Daily Mail*, October 7, 2010, http://www.dailymail.co.uk/news/article-1318381/Ikea-furniture-accounts-cent-household-items-UK.html.

48   Technically, Kamprad and his family do not own IKEA. In 1982, Kamprad founded Stichting INGKA as a charitable Dutch foundation intended to revolutionize architecture and interior design. Kamprad donated 100 percent of the equity in his company to the foundation, which not only relinquished his ownership of IKEA but also created the world's biggest charity, surpassing even the Bill and Melinda Gates Foundation. Still, Kamprad asserts that he retains the title of Senior Advisor for the company. Since Stichting INGKA is considered a Dutch charity, it is not required to pay taxes even for the revenue gained from the IKEA business.

49   In spring of 2012, IKEA stores began offering home delivery, beginning at $99. When contacted, spokeswoman Mona Liss declined to say what percentage of IKEA customers are opting for this service.

50   In October 2012 the IKEA group pledged to produce as much energy as it consumes by 2020 through a $1.95 billion investment in solar and wind projects. Officials said in a news release "the 'People and Planet Positive' plan is designed to protect the company from price shocks and tap into customers' desire for a greener lifestyle." Several

non-energy-centric goals in the new initiative include sourcing 50% of the company's wood supply from Forest Stewardship Council (FSC) -certified forests by 2017, helping to reduce supplier's carbon emission 20% by 2015, and sourcing cotton that meets the standards of the Better Cotton Initiative.

51   David Goldhill, "How American Health Care Killed My Father," *The Atlantic*, September 2009, http://www.theatlantic.com/magazine/archive/2009/09/how-american-health care-killed-my-father/307617/. After the needless death of his father, the author, a business executive, began "a personal exploration of a health care industry that for years has delivered poor service and irregular quality at astonishingly high cost. It is a system, he argues, that is not worth preserving in anything like its current form".

52   The spotlight on luxury accommodations comes at an awkward time for many urban hospitals, now lobbying against cuts in Washington and highlighting their role as nonprofit teaching institutions that serve the poor. Indeed, New York-Presbyterian, which once opposed amenities units, would not answer questions about its shift and declined a reporter's request for a tour (Nina Bernstein, "Chefs, Butlers, Marble Baths: Hospitals Vie for the Affluent," *New York Times*, January 21, 2012).

53   Nina Bernstein, "Chefs, Butlers, Marble Baths: Hospitals Vie for the Affluent," *New York Times*, January 21, 2012.

54   Including my older brother Bob, who in 2010 had surgery to remove a rare Klatskin tumor (cancer of the bile duct), which comes with a dire prognosis of a two-year survival rate. After six weeks in the hospital, with chemo, radiation, and excellent care, he is now back to his pre-surgery weight, back at work, and looking forward to dancing at his daughter's wedding. He was treated in the same hospital in which my father died.

55   Ken Schwartz, "A Patient's Story" *Boston Globe Magazine*, July 16, 1995.

56   Chip Health and Dan Heath *Switch: How to Change Things When Change is Hard,* Broadway Books, 2010, p. 79.

57   From "Increasing Patient Satisfaction: A Key Benefit of Improving Patient Flow Performance," a white paper published by the Stockamp Consulting Group.

58   My own do-it-yourself IKEA experience harkens back to my middle child's second year of college. After extracting the appropriate pieces from the IKEA store in Montreal, our division of labor left me facing several large cardboard boxes, armed only with a steak knife to slit open the boxes and a burning conviction that furnished apartments were underrated. Two hours later, the others returned and cooed appropriately over the fully assembled computer chair, kitchen table, and two chairs. No one was more surprised than I was.

59   Sandra G. Boodman, "Many Americans Have Poor Health Literacy," *The Washington Post,* February 28, 2011.

60   "To Promote Understanding, Assume Every Patient Has a Health Literacy Problem," ISMP.org, http://www.ismp.org/newsletters/acutecare/articles/20011031_2.asp.

61   The nonprofit Pew Internet Project says 75 percent of adults and 95 percent of teenagers in the United States have Internet access. However, adults living with chronic disease are significantly less likely than healthy adults to access the Internet: 64 percent of adults living with one or more chronic disease go online, while 81 percent of adults reporting no chronic diseases go online.

62   Healthcentric Advisors administers Medicare in the state of Rhode Island. At the time of this writing Gravenstein was also Professor of Medicine and Health Services Policy and Practice at Alpert Medical School of Brown University. His work on reducing hospital readmission won a prestigious Picker Institute "Always Event" Challenge Grant in 2012.

63   The Patient Pod (www.thepatientpod.com) is a hospital-tested device created by the author to improve the patient's safety and experience of care. Its role as an adjunct to "teach-back," minimizing harm during care transitions by engaging patients to manage their care post-discharge, will be explored in 2013.

64   Says Gravenstein, "The Patient Pod could provide a platform for this [ask-back], and a written attestation [write-back], rather than just a

verbal nod, as to what the patient and caregiver understand about what they're to do next."

65 Tejal K. Gandhi and Thomas H. Lee, "Perspective: Patient Safety beyond the Hospital," *New England Journal of Medicine* 363(11) (2010): 1001-1003.

66 From the company website: http://www.pgsi.com/Products/ProLingua.aspx.

67 The Medicare and Medicaid EHR (electronic health records) Incentive Programs provide a financial incentive for the "meaningful use" of certified EHR technology to achieve health and efficiency goals. By putting into action and meaningfully using an EHR system, providers "will reap benefits beyond financial incentives—such as reduction in errors, availability of records and data, reminders and alerts, clinical decision support, and e-prescribing/refill automation" (CMS EHR Meaningful Use Overview, cms.gov, accessed July 17, 2012).

68 Nancy Gibbs and Amanda Bower, "Q: What Scares Doctors? A: Being the Patient," *Time*, April 23, 2006.

69 Jay Elliot, *The Steve Jobs Way*, Vanguard Press, page 167.

70 *Health Affairs* is health policy journal publishing original, peer-reviewed research and commentary.

71 David Lansky, "Public Reporting of Health Care Quality: Principles For Moving Forward," HealthAffairsBlog.org, April 9, 2012.

72 From the 2011 keynote at the Medicine 2.0 Conference at Stanford University.

73 David "Doc" Searles, "The Patient as the Platform," *Linux Journal*, June 24, 2008, http://www.linuxjournal.com/content/patient-platform.

74 From the e-Patients.net website, http://e-patients.net/about-e-patientsnet.

75 CNN, December 15, 2011.

76 Graves related his story in a TEDMed Talk in October 2011.

77 The Swiss Cheese model of accident causation was originally propounded by British psychologist James T. Reason of the University of Manchester in 1990 (Reason 1990), and has since

gained widespread acceptance and use in healthcare, in the aviation safety industry, and in emergency service organizations.

78   The early verdict is in: both patients and physicians experimenting with an "open notes" policy at several hospitals of different sizes and demographics gave the concept a resounding "thumbs-up", according to a report published in October 2012 in the Annals of Internal Medicine.   http://www.rwjf.org/en/research-publications/find-rwjf-research/2012/10/inviting-patients-to-read-their-doctors—notes.html.

79   Such as "Hourly Rounding"; in this initiative developed by Studer Group consulting, care staff visit each patient on the hour to check on the four "P's"—Pain, Position, Potty and Possessions). Visit http://www.studergroup.com/flash_hourlyrounding.

80   Information confirmed to the author by many sources within several hospital systems. Even from a purely economic viewpoint, how can a patient who loses dentures, hearing aids or other important personal items in the hospital be satisfied with their hospital experience?

81   Some hospitals and nursing homes "lock up" patients' hearing aids or important personal items, so they won't get lost. This is time-consuming, inefficient, and disempowering for the patient.

82   In spring of 2012 IKEA stores began offering home delivery, beginning at $99. An IKEA spokeswoman declined to reveal what percentage of customers are choosing this option, saying the service is very new.

83   Though IKEA founder Ingvar Kamprad is noted for his frugality, he does allow himself some luxuries. He owns a villa in an up-market part of Switzerland, a large country estate in Sweden, and a vineyard in Provence, France. Document9

84   See website of the Society for Participatory Medicine (participatorymedicine.org), "bringing e-Patients together with health care professionals," and its blog, e-patients.net.

85   Jennifer Leigh Parker, "At-Work Wellness Boosts the Bottom Line," cnbc.com, January 24, 2012.

86 Michael I. Norton, Daniel Mochon, Dan Ariely, "The IKEA Effect, When Labor Leads to Love", *Journal of Consumer Psychology,* Volume 22, Issue 3, July 2012, Pages 453–460.

87 The global economic impact of the five leading chronic diseases— cancer, diabetes, mental illness, heart disease, and respiratory disease—could reach *$47 trillion* over the next twenty years, according to a study by the World Economic Forum (WEF). That's about 4 percent of the United States' annual GDP.

88 "Six Things Patients Do That Frustrate Their Doctors," ABC News. com, June 22, 2009, http://abcnews.go.com/Health/WellnessNews/ story?id=7884555&page=3#.T_Jnl-1uG5Q.

89 Rosalind Miller, "Revolutionizing Health Care for the Poor," *The Guardian,* January 21, 2011, http://www.guardian.co.uk/global-development/2011/jan/21/india-low-cost-healthcare.

90 Geeta Anand, "The Henry Ford of Heart Surgery," *Wall Street Journal,* November 25, 2009.

91 Rosalind Miller, "Revolutionizing Health Care for the Poor," *The Guardian,* January 21, 2011, http://www.guardian.co.uk/global-development/2011/jan/21/india-low-cost-healthcare.

92 Atul Gawande, "Doctor's Orders: Don't Stay Alone in the Hospital," Bigthink.com, January 19, 2010, http://bigthink.com/ideas/18218.

93 Domenic Frosch, Suepattra G. May, Katharine A.S. Rendle, Carolone Tietbohl and Glyn Elwyn, Authoritarian Physicians And Patients' Fear Of Being Labeled 'Difficult' Among Key Obstacles To Shared Decision Making, *Health Affairs, May 2012 vol. 31 no. 5 1030-1038.*

94 Email from Martin Hatlie to the author, October 14, 2012.

95 Email from Mary Ellen Mannix to the author, September 1, 2012.

96 Email from John James to the author, September 18, 2012.

97 Helen Haskell, Mary Ellen Mannix, John T. James, and David Mayer, "Parents and Families as Partners in the Care of Pediatric Cardiology Patients," *Progress in Pediatric Cardiology* 33 (2012), pp. 67-72.

98 Excerpted from Haskell et al, "Parents and Families as Partners in the Care of Pediatric Cardiology Patients," *Progress in Pediatric Cardiology* 33 (2012), pp. 67-72.

99 From a study in the *Journal of the American Medical Association.*

100 Froma Harrop, "Expensive Care That Hurts Patients", *Nation of Change*, March 21, 2012 http://www.nationofchange.org/expensive-care-hurts-patients-1332338890.

101 Maria Bartiromo, "Bartiromo: Top Doc at Cleveland Clinic Defends Health Care," *USA Today*, October 18, 2011, accessed online August 31, 2012, http://www.usatoday.com/money/companies/management/bartiromo/story/2011-10-14/cleveland-clinic-steven-nissen/50796928/1.

101 Gibson is co-author with Janardan Prasad Singh of *The Treatment Trap (Rowman & Littlefield, 2010), Wall of Silence: The Untold Story of the Medical Mistakes that Kill and Injure Millions of Americans (LifeLine Press, 2003)*, and *The Battle Over Health Care: What Obama's Reform Means for America's Future* (Rowman & Littlefield April 2012).

102 This information deserves a wider, mainstream audience; but media exposure hinges on naming names, and people going on the record. Gibson tells me she and others are working on this.

103 The Leapfrog Group is made up of leaders from 170 large companies publishing data on hospital performance, so consumers can shop and drive a market for improvement. Its current project is the Hospital Safety Score, a letter grade assigned to hospitals rating their propensity for errors, accidents, and injuries (www.hospitalsafetyscore.org).

104 Leah Binder, "What We Can Learn From Walmart: How Our Healthcare System Can Save Lives and Dollars", Forbes.com, October 17, 2012.

105 Tom Main, Adrian Slywotzky, "The Quiet Healthcare Revolution", *The Atlantic*, November 2011.

106 Bruce Japsen, "Small Picture Approach Flips Medical Economics", *NY Times*, March 12, 2012.

107 Bruce Japsen, "Obamacare's Accountable Care Approach Reaches 1 in 10 In U.S.", Forbes.com, November 26, 2012.

108 Rosemary Gibson, Janardan Prasad Singh, *The Battle Over Health Care: What Obama's Reform Means for America's Future*, Rowman & Littlefield Publishers, Inc., p. 104.

109 David Goldhill, "How American Health Care Killed My Father," *The Atlantic*, November 2009.

110 Steve Lopez, "The Bizarre Calculus of Emergency Room Charges," *The Los Angeles Times,* March 31, 2012.

111 Andrew Conte and Luis Fábregas, "Costs Can Vary Widely for Same Medical Procedures", *Pittsburgh Tribune,* September 25, 2011, http://triblive.com/x/pittsburghtrib/news/s_758618.html?_s_icmp= NetworkHeadlines#axzz2IcQ7bOYG*Pittsburgh Tribune-Review*.

112 David Wong via e-mail to the author, August 21, 2012.

113 "Global Players: Ingvar Kamprad, Founder and Senior Advisor, IKEA," Thomas White Global Investing, September 20, 2011, http://www.thomaswhite.com/explore-the-world/global-players/ ingvar-kamprad.aspx.

114 Trying to defuse criticism about the opacity of IKEA's corporate structure, which contrasts with its socially conscious image, the company in 2010 began publishing detailed figures on sales, profits, assets, and liabilities for the first time ever. Over the years the company has also been accused of using child labor in Asia (after a Dutch documentary on child labor in rug making in Asia aired, naming IKEA as a customer, the company terminated the Pakistan contract and put its own inspectors in place elsewhere). In 2009 it was accused of buying feathers plucked from live geese (the China supplier accused denied it, but IKEA phased out that line and cancelled orders). Journalists revealed that Mr. Kamprad had backed a Swedish fascist group in his youth; he apologized in an open letter. As *The Economist* writes: "When damaging news breaks, IKEA has an admirable habit of coming clean."

115 Claire Wilson, "Home Sweet Office for Ikea's Workers", *New York Times,* February 11, 2007, http://www.nytimes.com/2007/02/11/ realestate/commercial/11sqft.html?pagewanted=all.

116 *Ibid.*

117 Anna Jonsson, "Knowledge across Borders: A Study in the IKEA World," Lund University School of Economics and Management in Sweden, dissertation, 2008.

118 New ACGME duty hours regulations, which took effect in July 2011, now prohibit interns from working shifts of more than sixteen

hours. The ACGME is responsible for the accreditation of post-MD medical training programs within the United States.

119 "Intimidation: Practitioners Speak Up about This Unresolved Problem (Part I)," ISMP Medication Safety Alert! (March 11, 2004). Also available at http://www.ismp.org/MSAarticles /intimidation. htm (accessed May 12, 2004).

120 Ibid., plus "Intimidation: Mapping a Plan for Cultural Change in Healthcare (Part II)," ISMP Medication Safety Alert! (March 25, 2004). Also available at http://www.ismp.org /MSAarticlesfintimidation. htm (accessed May 12, 2004).

121 http://www.reuters.com/article/2013/02/05/pa-ross-feller-casey-idUSnPnPH54472+160+PRN20130205.

122 Rosemary Gibson, Janardan Prasad Singh, *The Battle Over Health Care: What Obama's Reform Means for America's Future*, Rowman & Littlefield Publishers, Inc., p. 111.

123 *Ibid*, p. 117.

124 Ben Goldacre, "Health Care's Trick Coin", New York Times Op-Ed, February 1, 2013. http://www.nytimes.com/2013/02/02/opinion/health-cares-trick-coin.html?ref=opinion&_r=0.

125 I've had the opportunity to be in the audience on two occasions to hear this story from the Malizzos and Tim McDonald, and to speak with them about their team approach to patient safety.

126 John Commins, Health Leaders Media: Learning From a Nightmare", December 13, 2012, http://www.healthleadersmedia.com/page-3/QUA-286741/HL20-Bob-MalizzomdashLearning-From-a-Nightmare.

127 Carolyn M. Clancy, MD, "Revealing Medical Errors Helps Chicago Hospitals Build a Safer Health System", July 10, 2012, AHRQ, http://www.ahrq.gov/consumer/cc/cc071012.htm.

128 Brian Goldman, "Doctors make mistakes", filmed at Tedx Toronoto in November 2011. http://www.ted.com/talks/brian_goldman_doctors_make_mistakes_can_we_talk_about_that.html#986000.

129 Boothman developed a pioneering approach to medical mistakes and risk management, one emphasizing an honest approach to errors, early apology, and rapid settlement offers when the system

was at fault. This approach, which has been demonstrated to lower malpractice payouts, has been emulated widely.

130   Interview of Rick Boothman by Robert Wachter, MD, on AHRQ website, accessed August 30, 2012, http://webmm.ahrq.gov/perspective.aspx?perspectiveID=117.

131   Philip Levitt, MD, "The American Medical Establishment Is on the Wrong Track in Its Efforts to Reduce Medical Errors," Axisoflogic. com, May 14, 2012.

132   Reached via email to comment on this report, Robert Oshel responded on October 3, 2012: "I didn't redo the numbers, but the first two bullet points seem correct. The fifty years comment in the last one concerns me though. It assumes a total of 625,000 physicians. I think 850,000 is a better estimate [see: Aaron Young, et al.; A Census of Actively Licensed Physicians in the United States, 2010. Journal of Medical Regulation, Vol 96, no. 4, 2011]. Secondly, it assumes that each physician has only one license and that removing that license would take him/her out of practice. In fact, the Young article cited says 22.7 percent of physicians are licensed in more than one state; indeed 5.9 percent are licensed in three or more states. Unless every state licensing a physician revokes his/her license when the first state does—which doesn't happen—many could keep practicing somewhere despite losing a license. Also some states grant new licenses to physicians who have lost a license elsewhere. So the situation is actually worse than suggested by Dr. Levitt."

133   Reached by email, Dr. Leape declined to comment.

134   E-mail from Rick Boothman to the author, May 16, 2012.

135   Robert M. Wachter and Peter J. Pronovost, "Balancing 'No Blame' with Accountability in Patient Safety," *New England Journal of Medicine,* October 1, 2009.

136   Penelope Green, "Romancing the Flat Pack: IKEA, Repurposed," *The New York Times,* September 6, 2007.

137   The study (*Infection Control and Hospital Epidemiology* 30, no. 6 (2009): 515-7) found a decrease in *C. diff* contamination of 50 percent after hypochlorite (bleach) decontamination and 91 percent after hydrogen-peroxide decontamination—which would make

hydrogen peroxide nearly doubly effective. I shared this information with two physicians who are infection-prevention specialists; they responded that the technology "has potential," but another, more recent study says "the requirement for both a pre-clean before use and the limited 'in vivo' evidence means that extensive field trials are necessary to determine their cost-effectiveness in a health care setting." Both studies relate to using hydrogen peroxide mist in the room, as opposed to wipes (which would arguably address pre-cleaning). (I also think it begs the question—why not do some studies? People are dying!) Meanwhile, the Lambert family kept Amy's *C. diff* (which is commonly ingested through hand-to-mouth contact) from infecting her husband or baby daughter by cleaning the surfaces in their one bathroom with 3% hydrogen peroxide, and powdered Oxiclean (a combination of powdered hydrogen peroxide and sodium carbonate) in the toilet bowl. FYI, the Clorox Company in March 2012 unveiled new patented hydrogen peroxide wipes and spray to sanitize health care environments. Stay tuned.

138 Tim Manners, "Key of IKEA," HubMagazine.com, September 2, 2007, http://www.hubmagazine.com/html/2009/jan_feb/ikea.html.

139 Joe Flower, *Healthcare Beyond Reform: Doing It Right for Half the Cost* (Productivity Press, 2012).

140 David Ewing Duncan, "Destroying Medicine to Rebuild It: Eric Topol on Patients Using Data," *The Atlantic,* March 12, 2012.

141 Joshua Schwimmer, MD, FACP, FASN, "Why Physicians Don't E-mail Patients," Healthline.com, April 12, 2012.

142 J. Goldsmith, "Healthcare IT's Unfulfilled Promise: What We've Got Here Is Failure to Communicate," in *Futurescan 2010*: Healthcare Trends and Implications 2010-2015 (Health Care Administration Press, 2010).

143 Pamela Hartzband, MD, and Jerome Groopman, MD, "Off the Record—Avoiding the Pitfalls of Going Electronic," *Journal of the American Medical Association,* April 17, 2012.

144 Arezu Servestani, "Healthcare is Grossly Engineered says John Hopkins' Pronovost (Podcast), January 18, 2013,MassDevice.com,

http://www.massdevice.com/features/healthcare-grossly-under-engineered-says-johns-hopkins-pronovost-podcast.

146 Rosemary Gibson, Janardan Prasad Singh, *The Battle Over Health Care: What Obama's Reform Means for America's Future*, Rowman & Littlefield Publishers, Inc., p. 112.

147 "A Simple Lesson for Patient-Centered Care," Hospitals & Health Networks, http://www.hhnmag.com/hhnmag/jsp/articledisplay.jsp?dcrpath=HHNMAG/Article/data/07JUL2012/0712HHN_Ahavoices&domain=HHNMAG.

148 Laura Landro, "The Simple Idea That Is Transforming Health Care," *The Wall Street Journal*, April 16, 2012.

149 Says Katharine White "Our three-fold approach includes coaching on wellness "best practices" so you can avoid hospitals (and attendant medical harm) entirely; immediate advocacy and support 24/7 for any hospitalization or care transition; and a patented seven-point activation science to get to the root of what transformational health outcomes you want, why you want them and how best to get you there." The author spoke with the Whites several times in August 2012.

150 Conversation between the author and Bill and Katharine White, August 2012.

151 Peter Pronovost, "Dreaming the Dream", *Points from Pronovost*, Johns Hopkins Blog, March 6, 2012, http://armstronginstitute.blogs.hopkinsmedicine.org/2012/03/06/dreaming-the-dream/.

152 Chip Heath and Dan Heath, *Switch: How To Change Things When Change is Hard*, Broadway Books, 2010, page 21.

153 Berwick left IHI in 2010 to take a recess appointment as Administrator of the Centers for Medicare and Medicaid. Sixteen months later he resigned because of heavy Republican opposition to his appointment and his potential inability to win a confirmation vote. He's now with a Washington think tank. As of January 2013 he was reportedly contemplating a run for Governor of Massachusetts.

154 Peter Pronovost, MD PhD, and Robert Wachter, MD, "The 100,000 Lives Campaign: A Scientific and Policy Review", Joint Commission

Journal on Quality and Patient Safety, November 2006, Volume 32, Number 11.

155   Peter Pronovost, MD PhD, and Robert Wachter, MD, "The 100,000 Lives Campaign: A Scientific and Policy Review", Joint Commission Journal on Quality and Patient Safety, November 2006, Volume 32, Number 11.

156   The six patient safety interventions of the campaign have evolved to become "best practices". They've been incorporated into a variety of quality initiatives, including the work of the Partnership for Patients. The number of lives that have been saved each year through these interventions since the campaign was completed is unclear.

157   Elizabeth Weitzman, NY Daily News, October 4, 2012, http://www.nydailynews.com/entertainment/tv-movies/movies-v-h-s-escape-fire-house-i-live-article-1.1175010#ixzz28eTZ7hpw.

158   Tom Delbanco, MD*; Jan Walker, RN, MBA*; Sigall K. Bell, MD; Jonathan D. Darer, MD, MPH; Joann G. Elmore, MD, MPH; Nadine Farag, MS; Henry J. Feldman, MD; Roanne Mejilla, MPH; Long Ngo, PhD; James D. Ralston, MD, MPH; Stephen E. Ross, MD; Neha Trivedi, BS; Elisabeth Vodicka, BA; and Suzanne G. Leveille, PhD, RN, "Inviting Patients to Read Their Doctors' Notes: A Quasi-experimental Study and a Look Ahead", *Annals of Internal Medicine*, October 2, 2012, http://annals.org/article.aspx?articleid=1363511.

159   Richard A. Knox, Doctor's Orders Killed Cancer Patient. Boston Globe. March 23, 1995L A1

160   Susan Brink. "Tragedy at Dana-Farber: Betsy Lehman's shocking death is still roiling the medical community", July 16, 1995. Accessed at: http://health.usnews.com/usnews/health/articles/950724/archive_032493_print.htm.

161   Scott Allen. "With work, Dana-Farber learns from '94 mistakes", Boston Globe. November 30, 2004. A1.

162   James B. Conway and Saul N. Weingart, "Organizational Change in the Face of Highly Public Errors", The Dana-Farber Cancer Institute Experience. AHRQ WebM&M. May, 2005. Accessed at: http://www.webmm.ahrq.gov/perspective.aspx?perspectiveID=3.

163 Christopher P. Landrigan et al., "Temporal Trends in Rates of Patient Harm Resulting from Medical Care", N Engl J Med 2010; 363:2124-2134 (November 25, 2010).

164 L. Millenson. "Why We Still Kill Patients: Invisibility, Inertia and Income", Health Affairs blog. December 6, 2010. Accessed at: http://healthaffairs.org/blog/2010/12/06/why-we-still-kill-patients-invisibility-inertia-and-income/; Dan C. Krupka, Warren S. Sandberg and William B. Weeks. The Impact On Hospitals Of Reducing Surgical Complications Suggests Many Will Need Shared Savings Programs With Payers. Health Affairs. Published online before print, October 2012. Accessed at: http://content.healthaffairs.org/content/early/2012/10/12/hlthaff.2011.0605.full.

165 Michael L. Millenson, "Why 3 Hospitals Didn't Hurt My Wife", The Health Care Blog, June 12, 2011. Accessed at: http://thehealthcareblog.com/blog/2011/12/06/why-three-hospitals-didnt-hurt-my-wife/.

166 Charles Andel et al, "The Economics of Health Care Quality and Medical Errors", Journal of Health Care Finance 2012; 39(1). Accessed at: http://www.mediregs.com/economics_of_quality_care.

167 The information contained in this document is informational only and is not intended to replace a doctor's advice. Pear Health LLC and its affiliates assume no responsibility for actions taken based on the information contained herein. Consult with your doctor about any health concerns.

168 Tips 18-22 are from Dr. Robert Wachter's book *Understanding Patient Safety* (a national leader in the fields of patient safety and healthcare quality). They can help you avoid medical error.

169 As reported in a 2009 study published in the *Archives of Internal Medicine*, surveying 449 internists and family practitioners.

170 As reported in a 2002 study published in *The Journal of Family Practice*.

CPSIA information can be obtained at www.ICGtesting.com
Printed in the USA
LVOW131941120613

338259LV00013B/1315/P